Afro-American Studies
by Nathan I. Huggins

A REPORT TO THE FORD FOUNDATION

One of a series of reports on activities supported
by the Ford Foundation. A complete list of publications may be obtained from the Ford
Foundation, Office of Reports, 320 East 43 Street,
New York, New York 10017.

**Library of Congress Cataloging in
Publication Data**
Huggins, Nathan Irvin, 1927–
  Afro-American studies.

  Includes bibliographical references.
  1. Afro-Americans—Study and teaching
(Higher)—United States.   I. Ford Foundation.
II. Title.
E184.7.H8 1984 305.8'96073'0071173 84-24714
ISBN 0-916584-25-9

Preface

Since 1969 the Ford Foundation has granted almost $30 million for the study of Afro-American, Hispanic, and Native American history and culture. This support reflects our belief that the rich experience of these groups has played an important part in the evolution of American society and that students as well as the larger public would benefit from knowledge of it.

The Foundation began by helping a few strong institutions—among them Howard, Princeton, Rutgers, Stanford, and Yale—to develop undergraduate programs in Afro-American studies. Subsequently, support was expanded to include Hispanic and Native American studies, and the grant focus shifted to the graduate level to train minority scholars and to add to scholarship about minority cultures.* Currently, the Foundation makes grants to advance the careers of minority scholars at the postdoctoral level and to strengthen selected research centers and ethnic archives.

Since Afro-American studies has accounted for nearly 50 percent of the total granted by the Foundation for ethnic studies, it seemed appropriate for the Foundation to review developments in the field. In 1982 therefore, the Foundation asked Nathan Huggins, director of the W.E.B. DuBois Institute for Afro-American Research at Harvard

---

*An account of these earlier programs is contained in *Widening the Mainstream of American Culture*, a Ford Foundation Report on Ethnic Studies, available upon request.

3

University, to survey the current status of Afro-American studies on American campuses in light of the early experience and future needs of the field. The report that follows is the result of that investigation.

A distinguished Afro-American scholar (his books on Frederick Douglass, on American slavery, and on the cultural flowering of Harlem are widely used references), Professor Huggins begins his report by placing the rise of the black studies movement within the context of the huge postwar growth of American higher education and of black demands for social justice. He describes the effort to gain a place for black studies in the curriculum as part of a broader movement to integrate black students and faculty into a traditionally white educational system. Strong programs were established in a number of institutions, with the result that by the 1980s few scholars any longer questioned whether the field was a legitimate subject for study. The aim now, Professor Huggins tells us, is to bring more sophisticated methodologies to bear on the study of black issues and to expand the presence of black studies in conventional disciplines.

Professor Huggins's report makes a valuable contribution to our understanding of an important chapter in American academic history, and the Foundation is pleased to publish it. We hope that it will serve as a guide and stimulus to other donors interested in aiding a scholarly initiative now well under way.

Susan V. Berresford
*Vice President, United States and
    International Affairs Programs
Ford Foundation*

Afro-American Studies

by Nathan I. Huggins

This essay—on the present state and future prospects of Afro-American studies—addresses what twenty years ago would have been considered two separate spheres of social concern: first, the growth and change taking place at American colleges and universities and, second, the struggle of blacks for social justice. During the late sixties these two spheres became interrelated; to some, indeed, inseparable. To understand Afro-American studies, a product of that period and of the interaction of those spheres, it is thus necessary to consider both American higher education and the American civil rights movement.

THE AMERICAN UNIVERSITY IN TRANSITION
In the quarter-century following World War II, the American university underwent enormous growth and a remarkable transformation. Both were unexpected. As late as 1941, Archibald MacLeish, referring to Harvard University, predicted "a period of organization within existing frontiers, rather than a period of extension of existing frontiers."[1] In less than a decade, all discussion of higher education in America was attempting to comprehend unprecedented expansion and transformation. By 1963, Clark Kerr's Godkin Lectures were defining the American university in new terms: as the multiversity or the federal-grant university.[2] Not only had it ballooned in size—numbers of students, faculty, and scale of physical plant—it had changed dramatically in char-

acter and purpose, departing both from Cardinal Newman's idealism and from the shaping influence of the German university.

Kerr merely articulated what had come to be commonly recognized: that the American university was no longer an academic cloister but was a major force in modern society—vital to industry, agriculture, medicine, government (in war and in peace), and social health and welfare. It was the major producer in what Kerr called the "knowledge industry," and crucial as such to economic and social progress and to national security. Perceiving itself (and generally being perceived) as essential to social and political change, the university naturally became an instrument for those demanding such change, blacks among them. To better understand the broader context of demands for black studies and the institutional response, we should consider aspects of this transformation of the university.

Growth

Between 1955 and 1965, the number of students (undergraduate and graduate) enrolled in U.S. colleges and universities more than doubled. The total of three million students enrolled during that one decade more than equaled the total number of students enrolled during the previous three *centuries* of American higher education. This extraordinary growth reflected more than the coming-of-age of the children of the postwar "baby boom." It was also a consequence of the democratization of higher education, a long-term trend in the United States but one that made a quantum leap when the G.I.'s came home following World War II. Ex-G.I. students embodied two important changes: the massive influx into higher education of people for whom such education had previously been possible (if even conceivable) only through city colleges and night schools, and direct federal support for tuition and expenses through the G.I. Bill. By the sixties, Americans shared two very new assumptions: that nearly everyone could benefit from some postsecondary educa-

6

tion and that everyone—without exception—was entitled to access to higher education. Chronic social inequities—in particular, the failure of one particular ethnic group, blacks, to move into the middle class—might, many thought, be explained by that group's systematic exclusion from most American colleges, universities, and professional schools.

While southern society in general, and southern, white universities and professional schools in particular, were early targets of the civil rights movement, northern institutions had been far from exemplary on racial matters. The liberal response to the demand of blacks for racial justice was, in part, to try to bring more black students into northern, white colleges and universities. The growth and democratization of the American university thus had racial consequences as well as those of class and scale.

Black migration northward and the G.I. Bill increased black enrollment in northern schools following World War II. From 1940 to 1950, the percentage of blacks residing outside the South increased from 23 to 32. C. H. Arce estimated that black enrollment in white colleges outside the South in 1947 was 61,000 (47 percent of all black enrollment but 3 percent of the total enrollment in those institutions). Black college enrollment was 6 percent of the total national enrollment that year, a rate not reached again until 1967.[3]

Between 1967 and 1971 black college enrollment increased enormously, by the latter year reaching 8.4 percent of total college enrollment. The numbers leveled off for two years and then began once again to grow, so that by October 1977 black enrollment accounted for 10.8 percent of total enrollment, a remarkable figure considering that in 1976 blacks made up 12.6 percent of the nation's 18-to-24-year-old, college-age population.[4] These increases were the result of aggressive recruitment by northern institutions and vastly increased financial aid, mainly from the federal government.

In the fifties, modest support for black students was

7

available through the National Scholarship Service and Fund for Negro Students. The funds of this group were later augmented by those of the National Defense Student Loan Program (1958) and the National Achievement Program (1964). The Higher Education Act of 1965 (Work Study, Educational Opportunity Grants, Guaranteed Student Loan Program) made additional funds available. These programs were followed in 1972 by the Basic Educational Opportunity Grant Program, which vested funds in individual students who could take them to the institutions of their choice. In 1976–77, $1.5 billion were awarded under this program, to nearly two million students. In addition to federal funds, state aid also became available. In 1977–78, for instance, there were $756 million in state-aid programs.

These figures point to an important characteristic of the growth of black student enrollment in the sixties. Not only did many more black students attend predominantly white schools in the mid-sixties; those who did were a different social slice of the black population than those who had attended those schools in the fifties and before. Administrators deliberately set out to recruit poor youngsters from the inner city (so-called ghetto youth), imagining that the university might rectify failures in the secondary-school system and redeem these students so they might enter mainstream life. This policy implied a changing (or at least a rethinking) of standards for admission as they applied to these youngsters. It implied the establishment of remedial programs, a faculty and a student body genuinely sympathetic both to the means and the ends of this policy, and inner-city black students who would be grateful for the opportunity. These assumptions were only partly to be realized, contributing to the general malaise among black students in the mid-sixties and leading in turn to much of the black contribution to student unrest in those years.

Being a black student at a predominantly white institution had never been easy. Before the sixties, such students had always been few in number, hardly more than a
8

dozen undergraduates at any time on any college campus. Sports and other extracurricular activities were sometimes closed to them. Little deference was given them, and they were likely to feel themselves alternately exemplars of their race and altogether ignored. Unlike those who arrived in the mid-sixties, however, they had not been specially recruited. Those who went to these institutions had made conscious, deliberate choices to be there, and had undoubtedly made important personal sacrifices. There had been no special admissions considerations, and they probably assumed (following conventional black wisdom) that they had to be better than whites to do as well. They expected to overcome obstacles and discrimination based on race. There could be a source of pride in that. It was pride as well (and their limited numbers) that made them unwilling to call attention to themselves by complaining even about real grievances.

After 1965, black college students were less likely to share these assumptions. Proportionately fewer were motivated in quite the same way; proportionately fewer had the educational background or the study habits to do well in these colleges. In addition, events outside the colleges—the war in Vietnam and, particularly, the continuing struggle for racial justice—were distracting from conventional academic pursuits. To some students—black and white—it seemed that the goals and values of those outside occurrences were in conflict with the university as it defined itself. Ironically, the growing number of black students contributed to their own malaise. There came a point, as their numbers grew, when their isolation became conspicuous. In earlier years, the handful of black students managed to fit in, badly or well, nursing as private matters any hurts they felt. With larger numbers, it became possible (indeed, almost inevitable) to consider being black on a white campus a collective condition. Private hurts became public grievances.

The extraordinary mid-century growth of the American university only partly explains the demand for black studies programs. Equally important were the assumptions about the new role of the university—assumptions about the university as a force extending social justice and its benefits to disadvantaged groups by means of higher education. The university would find it difficult to serve both traditional values and its new role of social reformer.

Shifting Academic Emphasis.
The American university had changed not only in size and purpose but in substance. The explosion of information, of new knowledge, had prompted Clark Kerr's metaphor of scholarship as "the knowledge industry." The new university was, of course, producing much of that new information; it was also training the engineers, technicians, and scientists who would put that knowledge to practical use in industry and government. One aspect of the university—science and technology—was experiencing dramatic growth, while the rest was being carried in its wake. The university was becoming, more than ever, the port of entry into the professions. The social sciences could help train young people to serve the expanding bureaucracies of government and industry. A natural consequence of these developments was the growing preprofessionalism of the undergraduate curriculum.

As faculty members and administrators saw the university in the terms defined by Kerr, as undergraduate teaching by research-preoccupied specialists became more problematic, and as the general public increasingly came to see higher education as training for careers, the pressure to make the undergraduate curriculum efficient to those ends became even more compelling. That efficiency, however, came at the expense of the liberal arts tradition. Public institutions, most having land-grant origins, from the beginning had appealed to their legislatures for funds by citing their immediate contribution to agriculture, mining, and business. They had always found it easy to design undergraduate curricula that allowed students to avoid "useless" courses in the humanities. In the postwar period, however, even the
10

prestigious private universities tolerated an erosion of the liberal arts core.

Kerr's utilitarian emphasis was echoed by most university administrators, most notably by James A. Perkins, president of Cornell.[5] By the end of the sixties, administrators and faculty were forced by both white and black students to defend themselves against charges of complicity in the evils of society and nation. Their defense relied heavily on the university's traditional posture of detachment and disinterest. "Relevance," a word often used by Kerr and Perkins to distinguish the modern university from the "ivory tower," became a student clarion call. Black students wanted courses and programs "relevant to our blackness," relevant to the lives of blacks in the ghettos and in the rural South. They wanted to make the university *useful* in ending racism in America (as others wanted to make it *useful* in ending poverty and the war in Vietnam). They would begin by confronting and excising the evil at the institution's heart. By the end of the hubristic sixties, university administrators and faculty were more than willing to recognize limits to their usefulness.

It is important to understand, however, that the emphasis on utility and relevance had already struck discordant notes among faculties, notes discordant with traditional views of the college and its curriculum. Utilitarianism seemed merely to emphasize the increasingly secondary place of the humanities in the university. Physics, and later biology and chemistry, were experiencing marked growth. (In those fields, far more than in any of the humanities, public and private funds were available for research and development, and national reputations could be made.) As the university was increasingly seen as the place for the creation of new knowledge and new techniques, the humanities were seen as less and less central. Social scientists and even humanists would mimic the physical and natural sciences, focusing ever more on methodologies and narrowing themselves into smaller and smaller specialties.

11

One of the principal characteristics of the liberal arts had always been *inutility*. The college graduate, according to the traditional conception, was not supposed to be able, on the basis of his education, to do anything; his education was, rather, supposed to do something to him. While faculty arguments over general education requirements often sounded suspiciously like squabbles over course enrollment (i.e., budget), matters of principle were at stake. Defenders of the liberal arts tradition found something superior in education for its own sake. John Henry Newman, in his *Idea of the University Defined* (1873), had characterized "useful knowledge" as a "deal of trash." The very process of distancing oneself from private concerns, of transcending mundane matters to glimpse the universal, was itself, he and many others felt, educational. Time enough later to train to make a living; some part of the postsecondary years should be given to training for life.[6] In contrast, James Perkins imagined that much of what passed for general education would, in the future, be taught in secondary school, where he thought it belonged.[7]

Given the new democratic and utilitarian direction of the American university, a defense of the humanities in terms of their inutility seemed perverse. That the strongest proponents of the liberal arts were to be found in expensive private schools tended to confirm the elitism of the humanities. It was difficult, also, to shake the Veblenian assessment that the pursuit of the liberal arts was merely an example of the conspicuous display of wealth; who else but the rich could afford to spend four years in pursuit of an education having no practical end? Humanists also easily drew the charge of elitism because they tended to think of their work as having a *civilizing* influence, and because their work (particularly in literature, the fine arts, and music) called upon them to make judgments as to quality. Some works were better than others; some writers, artists, and musicians were better than others. Those artists and works of art not studied, discussed, and evaluated were, by implication, inferior.

In practice, the liberal arts curriculum reduced itself to courses concerned with not just civilization, but *Western* civilization. Sometimes emphasis was placed on the "disciplines," sometimes on interdisciplinary approaches to "great issues," sometimes on the "great books" approach. The object was always the same: Matthew Arnold's "acquainting ourselves with the best that has been known and said in the world." Though the "world" of Matthew Arnold was small, it probably did include "acquaintance" with Islamic and Asian culture. Compared to Arnold's, the "world" of postwar American scholars in the humanities—products of university Ph.D programs—was Lilliputian. It certainly did not encompass Asia, Africa, and Latin America. Most American teachers in the humanities assumed *our* heritage (their students' as well as their own) to be the history and culture of the West. They could hardly imagine an American youngster of whatever ethnic background challenging that assumption.[8]

Most supporters of the liberal arts probably did not really believe that what they taught comprised the "world" or "civilization." Rather, they supposed certain concepts, ideals, principles, values, to be universal rather than particular to any people or culture. Those values were, nevertheless, accessible through certain texts and other cultural artifacts of a Western tradition, a tradition that could be studied as coherent and whole. *King Lear, Medea,* Machiavelli, Plato, Kant, Locke, Mill, Jefferson posed questions as relevant to a Chinese, a Malayan, a Ugandan, or a Nigerian as to an American of any ethnic background.

When, in the late sixties, black students challenged the curriculum, their main target was the parochial character of the humanities as taught. They saw the humanities as exclusive rather than universal. They saw humanists as arrogant white men in self-congratulatory identification with a grand European culture. To those students, such arrogance justified the charge of "racism."

The woeful ignorance of most humanists about all cultures and traditions other than their own made it difficult for them to respond to the charge in a constructive way. Nothing in the training of American scholars in the humanities—scholars who were becoming more and more specialized even within the tradition they knew and accepted—prepared them for the challenge. Not surprisingly, their response was dogmatic: what they taught was the best that could be taught; it was what truly educated men and women needed to know; it trained (that is, disciplined) the mind; it was *our* heritage.

The same defense had been raised against the utilitarians in the university. It is important to understand that black students were taking aim at the segment of the college that was already the most frequently attacked; theirs was merely the latest in a series of frontal assaults. To the embattled humanists, black students arguing for courses "relevant to our blackness" sounded much like engineering students demanding that they be exempted from courses not "relevant" to their professional training. Humanists thus saw themselves as holding the line against a new wave of Philistines. This time, however, the Philistines were poor and black, and, when not denouncing their courses as worthless, a deal of trash, they were demanding both remedial courses to help them read and write and the redesign of admission standards to make college more accessible to inner-city blacks with inadequate high school training.

The social science faculties were less central, but they, too, came under attack. Political scientists, sociologists, and economists had for some time been modeling themselves after the natural and physical scientists. Historical and "institutional" study had diminished in importance in these fields. Systems and model analysis had become dominant, and even theory had ceased to be broadly philosophical, becoming instead a matter of model definition and analysis. As positivists, social scientists tended to avoid *a priori* assumptions and value judgments; their mastery of sophisticated methodologies defined the objective condition of the subject under study, implying solutions.

14

Few social scientists took up questions having directly to do with Afro-American life and circumstances, and few courses offered could be said to have to do with blacks. Events outside the university nevertheless spoke loudly to the fact that questions regarding race were at the heart of American social, political, and economic problems. When social scientists discussed blacks at all, black students found, they often did so in pathological terms, asking why blacks had failed to move into the social mainstream more quickly. The most flagrant example was Daniel P. Moynihan's *The Negro Family*—the so-called Moynihan Report—which seemed to place the blame for continued poverty among blacks on a dysfunctional black family.[9]

Black students and scholars thus began to challenge the "objectivity" of mainstream social science. In most "scientific" discussions of "problems" a norm was assumed, that of the white middle class; the social scientist, himself, was at the center, defining all variation as deviation and "blaming the victim," as critics liked to say. The demand of black students was for a discussion of what they saw to be the inherent racism in these normative assumptions and for a shift in perspective that would destigmatize blacks and reexamine the "normalcy" of the white middle class.

Black students and their allies imagined that out of these demands—for the introduction of nonwhite subject matter into the curriculum and for the shift of normative perspective—would come a revolutionary transformation of the American university. It was a transformation that neither Clark Kerr nor James A. Perkins anticipated; but then they could not have predicted the course of the civil rights movement and its impact on the university.

THE BLACK STUDENT MOVEMENT
There are those who claim that the general unrest on college campuses in the sixties had roots in the movement of southern black students to bring about reforms for racial justice. Whether or not that is true, the general social pro-

tests of that decade shared assumptions and tactics with the black student movement: (1) the evils to be corrected were endemic to society and its institutions; (2) individuals who worked within society's institutions (within "the system") were, consciously or unconsciously, controlled by attitudes, conventions, and bureaucratic constraints that made reform either impossible or painfully slow ("freedom *now*" was the slogan); and (3) therefore, direct confrontation was necessary to bring Americans to see the urgency of radical change and to act.

The early tactics of such organizations as the Student Nonviolent Coordinating Committee (SNCC) and the Congress of Racial Equality were difficult to ignore. Young people putting their bodies and their lives in jeopardy for the cause of civil rights touched a central nerve of American idealism. The mass media brought their protests into every home, broadcasting to the world the ugly and persistent problem of racism in America. These students were agents of disorder; their nonviolence exposed the evil of their adversaries. The civil rights movement attracted whites as well as blacks from throughout the country, and much of its financial support came from northern white contributors.

The demand of black students for reform on college campuses was in their view an extension of the civil rights movement, transported from the South to the North (where racism was less overt but just as pernicious) and onto predominantly white college campuses. By the mid-sixties, when the movement manifested itself on northern college campuses, its tactics and assumptions had changed in important ways. The northern black students had come to question nonviolence. Change had been much too painful and slow, and achievements had been ambiguous. Most of the black students were from northern cities and thus were far removed from the influence of Christian stoicism in the southern black church. They attended the words of Malcolm X more than those of Martin Luther King, Jr., or of student nonviolent leaders. SNCC, itself, had changed by the middle of the decade. Its membership had come to question nonviolence as a tactic, resulting, by 1966, in a change of leaders from John Lewis to Stokely Carmichael. The change reflected the membership's growing militancy, their being tired of turning the other cheek, and a growing race-centered emphasis. Carmichael popularized the slogan "black power" and stressed the desire to place the movement in the hands of blacks. The removing of whites from leadership positions, the indifference to their presence and even their financial support, became the general attitude of blacks throughout the organization. In February 1968 three South Carolina State students were killed by police in Orangeburg; they had been using nonviolent tactics to desegregate a bowling alley. In April 1968, Martin Luther King, Jr., was assassinated. These events, and the rapidly changing mood and character of the black student movement, had more to do with the style and attitude of black students in northern schools than did the specific actions (or inaction) of individual administrators or faculty members.[10]

By the early sixties, most administrators and faculty members at northern universities willingly extended their assumptions about the social role of the university and its democratizing principles to include Afro-Americans. Few questioned assertions of the historic and systemic nature of racism in America, doubted the need for the admission of blacks to colleges and universities in order that they be incorporated into the American mainstream, or challenged the view of higher education as a principal instrument of upward mobility. Faced with the glaring inequities exposed by sit-ins and other protests, many, too, were willing to accept the necessity and efficacy of compensatory treatment of blacks (that is, modification of admission standards and expansion of remediation programs).

Recent experience supported the notion that high motivation could compensate for a weak secondary education. Many G.I.'s had proved that to be the case. The postwar experience of blacks in predominantly white schools proved it also. While they had been few in number, the blacks who went to northern schools in the forties and fifties had done well. Their dropout rate was much lower than the average, and their grade level was at least as high as their white peers. Those of that generation who responded to a survey generally described their college life as gratifying, often as the most important experience of their lives. They reported little racial antagonism or hostility, and they considered their treatment by administrators and professors to have been fair.[11]

One would have expected much the same from those black students arriving in increasing numbers after 1967. College was a great opportunity being opened to this class of Americans for the first time.[12] But if faculty members and administrators expected these students to be grateful and appreciative for the opportunity, they were disappointed. Increased numbers—the recruitment effort itself—effected a change in attitude and expectation. Fairly or unfairly, many black students attributed the institutions' efforts to increase their numbers to an attempt to assuage guilt for past and present racism. Many expressed themselves to the effect that their presence on campus benefited whites and their institutions rather than the other way around; many detected an attitude of condescension in the efforts of white liberals to uplift ghetto youth. Furthermore, as black students on a campus achieved a "critical mass," racial problems that might previously have been accepted as matters of private adjustment could be dealt with collectively. Larger numbers made another difference: black students saw whites—students, faculty, and community—as being threatened by their numbers, by their very life style. It was a time, after all, of open and symbolic displays of militancy. Hair styles, clothing, language, name changes all conspired to challenge and intimidate. The white response to black student demands was too often shocked and fearful uncertainty, which did little but increase the anxiety felt by blacks. Thus, one detects a similar cycle in every situation where there were confrontations by black

18

students: alienation expressed in terms of racial grievance, followed by ever more strident demands, answered by fearful and uncertain response, in turn provoking greater anxiety and alienation.

Between 1965 and 1970, black undergraduates became increasingly militant. Events outside the university had much to do with it, but it also seemed that each new freshmaɪ class was more militant than the one before, especially as students were increasingly drawn from the inner city. It is also the nature of student life always to be changing in leadership; each year, seniors with the wisdom of experience are lost at the top and replaced at the bottom by persons who have never before dealt with a complex bureaucracy. Perversely, however, it was the underclassmen who, in the sixties, challenged the leadership of seniors, demanding of them greater militancy.[13]

CRISIS OF ESTABLISHMENT

Between 1966 and 1970, most American colleges and universities added to their curricula courses on Afro-American life and history, and most made efforts to include blacks on their faculties and administrative staffs. The fact that schools like Macalester, Bowdoin, Colby, Reed, Dartmouth, and Carleton (to pick just a few names), which were relatively free of pressure, joined the rush argues that there was something more to explain it than the threat of students disrupting academic life. Like all other aspects of the movements for peace and civil rights, the demand for university reform by black students was national in its impact as well as local in particular manifestations. In some sense, the urge for change was everywhere; whether or not a campus had militant black students making demands, the urge for reform was in the air.

I suggest three motives, independent of immediate student pressure, that compelled college administrators and faculty to join the march for change. First, there was, particularly among liberal-minded academics, a genuine sense of American higher education's complicity in the

19

social inequities resulting from racism—indifference to black undergraduate enrollment, insensibility to non-white subject matter in the curriculum, and the discouragement of black scholars. Second, it had become fashionable to bring blacks onto staffs and faculties, just as it had earlier become fashionable to recruit "hard-core, inner-city kids" for admission. The sense of competition among institutions should not be discounted; the legitimate purpose of the act too often was joined by the wish to do at least as well as comparable institutions. Third, in their effort to attract the "best" applicants from a generation of teenagers noted for their social consciousness, college administrators felt it important to look reasonably open to change, to appear to be progressive without compromising integrity. A course or two on black history or culture could achieve that end.

The great majority of institutions added courses pertinent to Afro-Americans and, as a direct result or not, experienced little or no student disruption; most changes involved merely a course or two and could hardly be called a program in black studies. Yet, from 1966, student disorders were increasingly common, and no college or university could be indifferent to, or uninfluenced by, events at San Francisco State, Cornell, Harvard, Wesleyan, and so on. It was widely assumed that disruptions of the sort that had occurred at those institutions could be avoided, if at all, only by swift and significant reform.

With the spurt of black enrollment in 1966, students and administrators began a process of negotiation aimed at correcting the problems perceived by black students. One problem was that many black students felt themselves to be educationally disadvantaged compared to their white peers; they wanted remedial programs that would compensate for their poor high schools (poor because white society made them so) and poor study habits. Problems also arose because of a deep sense of alienation from the institutions and their goals. This alienation was often expressed by defining schools as "white," as a part of a "white, racist system." Blacks'
20

success and achievement within these institutions could come only if they "whitewashed their minds" and alienated themselves from "their people" and "their community." In this view, while college may have been a necessary route to upward mobility, success within the college would be purchased through the denial of one's "blackness" and through co-optation by the system. This was the black version of the widespread (and, among many young Americans, the rampant) alienation from mainstream, conventional, middle-class America. For black undergraduates, the solution to this dilemma was an assertion of blackness: beauty, culture, community, etc. The newly developing black student associations, therefore, pressed to make the college environment congenial and hospitable to what they described as black values and culture. They wanted student activities for black students, black cultural centers. Sometimes they asked for separate dormitories (or black floors or sections of dormitories); they established black tables in dining halls and treated white students with the same hostility and contempt they assumed whites had for them. They almost always pressed for the appointment of black faculty and for the introduction of courses "relevant to us as black people."

Black student leaders found some sympathetic ears among faculty members, administrators, and white students, but their demands also created hostility among the same groups. To some, the demand for remediation only supported the belief that standards were being lowered to admit black students who were bound either to fail or to undermine the quality of education. The new black assertiveness could only antagonize those who held to the ideal of integration and of a color-blind system of merit. Black students were, in their view, racists who merely wanted to turn an evil on its head. Antagonism over these issues set the tone for the debate over black studies when it became a central issue, and it also affected the reception of these programs when they were established by the end of the decade.

For the most part, negotiations went quietly. Colleges like Bowdoin, Carleton, Macalester, and Dartmouth, removed from crosscurrents of student radicalism, were able to move at their own pace to increase black enrollment, appoint black faculty and staff, and introduce a few courses on topics of interest to Afro-Americans.[14] In some conspicuous instances, however (Cornell, San Francisco State, Wesleyan), the students armed themselves, and the threat of riot and violence was quite real. At other institutions, calls for black studies courses and programs merely added to a general atmosphere of conflict and upheaval. To the most vociferous activists, Afro-American academic programs were likely to be of incidental or secondary importance; what they were really interested in was not an academic but a political revolution.

San Francisco State
On September 29, 1968, the trustees of the California State College System voted 85 to 5 to fire one G. M. Murray from his post as an untenured lecturer at San Francisco State College. Murray, a member of the Black Panthers, had been hired as part of an attempt to increase black faculty; he had been teaching courses that were, according to Murray, "related to revolution." The firing set in motion a series of shocks to the campus, including student strikes, violence from civilians and police, the closing of the school, and the final enforcement of order under the newly appointed president, S. I. Hayakawa.

The institution came as close to anarchy as one could possibly imagine, with college faculty and students, the mayor and citizens of San Francisco, Governor Ronald Reagan, and President Hayakawa engaged in strategies alternating between charges, threats, demands, the use of violence, naked power, and, from time to time, efforts at arbitration. Lines were firmly drawn, and few were willing to negotiate. In time, backed by Governor Reagan, Hayakawa succeeded in reopening the school much on his own terms.

Black studies, as an issue, was one element (but by no
22

means the most important) in the dispute. On December 7, 1968, the Black Student Union rejected Hayakawa's offer to establish a black studies department under the direction of Dr. Nathan Hare. The Black Student Union wanted a program with more "autonomy" than Hayakawa would permit, and there were elements in the union's demands suggesting a racially separatist model. Conflict between blacks and Hayakawa continued for nearly two years. On March 1, 1969, Hare announced that he had received a letter from Hayakawa stating that he would not be rehired in June. In June, four of the college's six black administrators resigned, charging Hayakawa with racism. On November 2, 1969, Hayakawa accused the black studies department of a "reign of terror" and threatened to disband it, claiming that it was both authoritarian and anarchistic. By Christmas 1969, he had again threatened to close it and to put worthy courses under other departments. The bickering continued until March 3, 1970, when the entire black studies faculty was ousted because the department's hiring, retention, and tenure committee reports were turned in only an hour before the deadline.[15]

Cornell University
The first evidence of serious racial discord at Cornell came as early as January 1968, when a black student successfully challenged the validity of a psychiatric examination that had been administered by a white person. In April of that year, black students protested the "covert racism" of a visiting professor of economics, Michael McPhelin. Getting no results from the economics department or the dean, the students disrupted McPhelin's class by reading a statement. This brought about a judicial action against the students, protests of the resulting punishments, and, finally, the occupation by a hundred black students of the student union building. The occupation of Willard Straight Hall occurred in April 1969, a full year after the initial event. In the course of this occupation, the students armed themselves and made a

series of demands, placing the negotiations with the faculty and administration in an atmosphere of imminent violence. The occupation ended as the students, armed with rifles, shotguns, and belts of ammunition over their shoulders, marched out of the building.

These were the most public and most notorious events; the struggle to establish a black studies program was going on simultaneously, as if it were a separate and independent matter. On September 15, 1968, the university agreed to establish an Afro-American studies program with a budget of $250,000 a year, and announced a search for notable black scholars to staff it. In early December, however, students from the Afro-American society met with the acting director of the program and insisted that the program be turned over to black students. Within a week they demanded that Afro-American studies be established as an autonomous all-black college.

President Perkins reaffirmed his support for an Afro-American studies program but rejected the idea of an all-black college. The faculty-student committee appointed James Turner, a graduate student, as director. In time, Turner was able to convince the faculty and administration that a separatist black-studies program made sense. By mid-May 1969, in the wake of the most potentially explosive racial conflicts ever on a northern campus, Cornell acquiesced. While the program was neither autonomous nor all-black, it was one of the most separatist and most political in the country.

University of California (Berkeley)
By the spring of 1969, the University of California at Berkeley had been shaken by a series of student protests, few having to do with minority issues. Yet increased numbers of minority students, and their heightened consciousness of special needs, brought pressure on the university to reform its curriculum and increase minority faculty. These demands (in a context of broad student demand for reform) resulted in the creation that spring of a department of ethnic studies, which was divided into
24

Afro-American, Chicano, contemporary Asian, and Native American studies divisions. The student instigators of this reform, behaving in keeping with the alienation they felt, insisted that the department remain outside the College of Letters and Sciences. In effect, they wanted to be a separate college, dealing on budgetary and other matters directly with the chancellor. They were especially concerned that the traditional disciplines (that is, the university faculty) should have no say about course content or faculty appointments.

Each division within the Department of Ethnic Studies developed differently. Native American studies has remained quite small. Chicano and contemporary Asian studies, while larger, has never developed a strong academic emphasis; the latter, in fact, has concentrated on "community outreach" rather than scholarly programs. The department's history has been marked by internal conflict among its divisions and, in its relations with the university, by conflicts over budget and autonomy. In all of the department's divisions, student participation in policy and management was assumed to be necessary. The Afro-American studies faculty, after some tumultuous years marked by internecine fighting (in 1969, faculty and students came armed to meetings) and an undefined academic program, left the ethnic studies department in 1974 and joined the College of Letters and Sciences.

In 1972, the university forced a change in the leadership of Afro-American studies by replacing its nontenured director with William M. Banks, a psychologist who was appointed with tenure. It was through Banks's leadership (despite student boycotts of Afro-American studies courses) that Afro-American studies elected in 1974 to join the College of Letters and Sciences as a normal university department. It has since become one of the stronger departments of its kind in the country, with several notable tenured faculty. It has been aided in this by the fact that some other departments at the university (notably, history) have long been offering courses on aspects of Afro-American life.[16]

Yale University

By all accounts, the Afro-American studies program at Yale is the strongest and most respected in the country. It has been a healthy program from the beginning, and that fact has much to do with the way it came into being: intelligent and wise leadership from faculty, students, and administration and a genuine spirit of cooperation among them. From the fall of 1967, the Black Student Alliance at Yale had been working, without much success, to convince the college of the need for courses in Afro-American history and culture. Early in the spring of 1968, they decided to sponsor a conference that would draw nationally upon white and black intellectuals having something to say about the subject. One of the student organizers, Armstead Robinson, has written: "We viewed this symposium as an opportunity to create an atmosphere in which those persons who were in pivotal positions...could engage in active and open intellectual exchanges on questions related to Afro-American studies."[17]

Supported by funds from the Ford Foundation, this symposium to educate the educators brought together a wide spectrum of opinion (all favorable to some form of Afro-American studies). Some, like Nathan Hare and the "cultural nationalist" Maulana Ron Karenga (of UCLA), were deeply anti-intellectual and hostile to the academy. These were offset by such self-conscious intellectuals and committed academics as Martin Kilson, Harold Cruse, and Boniface Obichere. The result was a provocative conference that gave the Yale community a chance to compare several differing concepts of black studies and to identify the one that might work best at Yale.

The development of the Yale program was helped most by the constructive attitude of the university's senior faculty and the deft leadership of its administration, out of which a program emerged that was an integral part of the life of the institution. Several of the major departments (including history, English, and anthropology) supplied faculty and courses to the program, and the administration allocated the funds to make that possible. Such a pro-

26

gram required trust and respect by all parties. Whatever the reasons that Yale had those qualities, they were hard to come by at other institutions. The result is that others have had to suffer painful periods of adjustment to get to the point at which Yale was able to start. After more than a decade, some are just now getting there.

Harvard University

Harvard's program might have gone the way of Yale's except for bad timing, bad luck, and perhaps excessive distrust on the part of some of those concerned. Like Yale, Harvard began working on the problem in the spring of 1968. The historian Frank Friedel had organized a successful course on the Afro-American experience.[18] A student-faculty committee under the chairmanship of Henry Rosovsky[19] was organized to report on a wide range of issues related to Afro-American student life and needs at Harvard. The committee made its report to the faculty in January 1969, recommending a program in Afro-American studies (one similar to that later adopted by Yale), increased graduate fellowships for black students, and a variety of measures to enhance black student life on campus. The student members of the Rosovsky committee were unable to win for the report the general approval of Harvard's black students. Nevertheless, the report was adopted by the faculty in February and a committee was established to implement it.

In just two months, however, everything had changed. On April 9, in a totally unrelated matter, student members of Students for a Democratic Society (SDS) and the Progressive Labor Party occupied University Hall demanding the banning of ROTC from the Harvard campus, the university's active commitment to ending the war in Vietnam, and amnesty for certain students who were under disciplinary terms from a previous demonstration. (In all, there were nine "non-negotiable demands," most without lasting significance.) The protesters at University Hall were mainly white students and the "sit-in" had nothing to do with black studies, but the

27

dramatic outcome of this demonstration was to radically change the context in which discussion of all reforms was to take place. It was a new ball game.

The police were called to force the eviction of the demonstrators and a general strike by students followed. The faculty met in the ensuing weeks to deal with a range of issues flowing from those student protests. There was justifiable concern among administrators, faculty, and students that the university could be shut down or forced to operate under a state of siege.

The leadership of the Association of African and Afro-American Students, becoming more militant (or more emboldened by the crisis atmosphere), presented the faculty with new demands framed as a thinly veiled ultimatum. They wanted Afro-American studies to be a department on its own and not a program, and they wanted a student voice in the selection and appointment of its faculty. On April 22, the faculty were asked to vote on these propositions without altering them. Although deeply divided, and despite the forceful opposition of Henry Rosovsky, Martin Kilson, and others, the faculty voted for the changes the students demanded. It was a bitter decision, as were many the faculty made in the days following. One could hardly expect an Afro-American studies department, thus created, to have the warm support from administration and faculty that the Yale program enjoyed.[20]

Wesleyan University
Until 1967, the number of black undergraduates at Wesleyan had been negligible. After that year, the numbers grew significantly. The change in racial composition resulted in serious and disturbing friction between white and black students in the fall and winter of 1969. In December 1969, the Ujamaa Society (the black student group) had to be restrained by court order from disrupting campus student events that the black students considered "white" and thus unrelated to the needs of black students. At Wesleyan, as at Cornell, the threat of violence was real.

To meet the demands of Ujamaa, Malcolm X House was established as a black cultural center and as a center for Afro-American studies. As we shall see, the program that emerged was confused in academic purpose.

Few academic institutions in the country had experiences as dramatic as Cornell's or Wesleyan's, but all with sizable numbers of black undergraduates faced similar demands for reform. Keeping peace on campus was everywhere a principal concern of faculty and administrators. Black students everywhere were making similar demands. These included: (1) increased recruitment of black students; (2) increased financial aid and special support for remedial needs; (3) an increased number of black faculty and advisers; (4) courses "relevant" to black and/or Third World peoples; (5) a black studies program (or department); (6) a black or Third World cultural center; (7) course credit or a program for community work. All of these items did not have the same weight everywhere, and institutions responded to them variously. It is important to recognize, however, that black studies was only one item in a package. It was not always the most important item to students, and it was not always feasible to implement.

The most difficult problem for all northern institutions was to find qualified (or even marginally qualified) black scholars. In 1970, a Ford Foundation survey revealed that less than one percent of Americans with doctorates were black, and that most of that one percent were more than fifty-five years old.[21] The sudden demand for black scholars increased anxiety among educators concerned about the future of southern black institutions. The fear was that northern schools would "raid" traditionally black colleges for the black academics who, for racial reasons, would hardly have been considered for membership in white departments before the 1960s.[22] Northern institutions would find it difficult to discover black candidates for faculty appointment, but they could and did funnel money to the support of black students, add black faculty or staff where they could, offer new courses in Afro-Ameri-

29

can history and literature, swallow liberal instincts by accepting de facto separate facilities under the guise of black culture, and put together what might be called a program in Afro-American (or African-American) studies. All of this in response to black student demands.

It is hard to know how much black students wanted Afro-American studies as a field for possible academic concentration. Doubtless much of their demand arose from their desire to shake the complacency of their institutions. In that sense, black studies was symbolic; its presence was more important than its substance. But it was also a field of legitimate scholarly inquiry, as black scholars have been saying for more than a century. Black studies, as fact and symbol, would continue to create tension among black scholars and student reformers because some black scholars wanted their scholarship to be taken seriously and were as likely to be put off by anti-intellectualism and hostility to academic work as were their white peers. We should consider more closely some of the reasons advanced for the establishment of these programs.

ASSUMPTIONS OF REFORM
In most institutions, black studies was part of a larger package of reforms insisted on by black students and their supporters among the reform-minded faculty and students. The demands for reform began with a general malaise among all students and particularly among blacks; I would suggest that the remedies they seized on were "in the air" rather than derived from specific needs in particular circumstances. I am persuaded in this by the near-uniformity of the demands nationally and by the adamantly collective character of the protest; there was little if any individual refinement or qualification. It is therefore hard to judge the significance of black studies to any particular campus. As we will see, there were many different expectations as to what black studies should be. It is worth reviewing some of the assumptions behind the demands. For the sake of clarity, I will discuss three dis-

tinct expectations, although they were generally confounded.

"To Have Something That Is Ours"
In striking contrast to the reported experience of black undergraduates in predominantly white schools in the fifties, blacks in college in the sixties felt racially alienated and isolated. It might seem that, because the earlier group was so small in number, its members should have felt isolated, but generally they reported fitting in. They differed also in that their admission to college was untainted by suspicions that it was attributable to special standards or compensatory policy. They were highly motivated to succeed in mainstream, middle-class America. They were likely to see their presence, success, and achievement in a white college as a sign of racial progress and thus uplifting. If they had a sense of alienation from whites or from the black community, they did not make their feelings public.[23]

Ironically, as the numbers of black students increased in the late sixties, the students increasingly reported that they were alienated and isolated from the rest of the campus. That, undoubtedly, had to do with a number of factors: (1) a large number of students were drawn from socioeconomic circumstances where the conventional academic expectations and values were weak or lacking; (2) the lowering of admissions standards to increase the number of black, inner-city youth enrolled was publicly acknowledged, encouraging those so admitted to regard themselves—and to be regarded—as second-class enrollees; (3) many black students were, in fact, poorly prepared for college, lacking adequate academic preparation, discipline, study habits, or all three; (4) many found college work not only difficult but uninteresting and irrelevant to their lives as black people; (5) many felt that the ultimate end of success in college would be adaptation to the values of conventional white America, and thus a placing of distance between themselves and other black people; (6) their larger numbers, rather than making

31

them feel more at home, gave them a collective sense of malaise and made it easy to divide the world into black and white; (7) greater numbers also meant peer-group pressure on those who otherwise might have adapted easily to join in the general malaise; (8) the institution in all its aspects—courses, student activities, facilities—could easily be divided into "theirs" and "ours."

Black students could call little of what normally existed at predominantly white institutions "ours." Much of the emotional energy of black student protest was aimed at forcing faculties and administrations (generally liberal and integrationist in values) to accept race differences in ways that guaranteed blacks a sense of "turf" while refraining from any racial distinctions suggestive of racism. While the student demands might have begun as requests for programs and activities "relevant to black people," with no implication of being exclusionary, they almost always evolved into de facto black dormitories, cultural centers, programs, etc. The few curious whites who ventured in were soon made to feel hostility against them and their alienation. Demands for black "turf" generally resulted in separatism. Students at San Francisco State (1968), U.C. Berkeley (1968), Cornell (1968-1969), Wesleyan (1970), and Barnard (1970) were, in fact, explicit in their demand for racially separate programs or facilities.

Little wonder that in such an atmosphere demands were heard for "courses relevant to us as black people." The standard curriculum's indifference to the special problems, concerns, and basic humanity of Afro-Americans and other non-Europeans seemed glaring. Socrates, Plato, Aquinas, Goethe, Kant, Hegel, Milton, Shakespeare, Donne, Eliot, Dylan Thomas, were all *theirs*, and *they* celebrated them. "Who are we?" black students asked. "What is ours?"

It was generally assumed that those questions could best be answered by courses on the African and Afro-American experience: on black history, literature, music, and "culture." For some, the informational content of

32

such courses was paramount. For others, course content was less important than the mere presence of such courses in the catalog. Students in the former group were likely to be more concerned with the quality of instruction than with the color of the instructors. Students in the latter group were likely to insist that only blacks were qualified to teach such courses; some even demanded all-black classes or sections.[24] Carrying such thinking to its logical end, some demanded complete academic "autonomy": a separate college (as was called for at Berkeley, San Francisco State, and Cornell) or a separate department (as was called for at Harvard). The indifference to course content and preoccupation with symbolism rather than substance of those in the latter group caused many black studies programs to be ridiculed and eventually abandoned by black students as well as white.[25]

Quest for Identity
Many black students on white campuses regarded the college experience as a threat to their sense of ethnic identity, and thus to their sense of personal identity.[26] Ironically, it was the very liberalization taking place in society —residential desegregation, greater prospects of upward mobility—that created the problem. In the past, blacks had all been pretty much in the same boat regardless of class and education. Now, black prospects included admission to a good college, a position—if only "token"— in corporate America, entry into the mainstream middle class, a move "out of the ghetto" and into the suburbs, and acceptance by conventional white America. Such "upward mobility," though attractive to many black students and increasingly common, was repugnant to others, who claimed that it cut black people off from the vast majority of their brothers and sisters and from their ethnic and cultural roots. The best way to guarantee one's personal identity, it seemed to many blacks, was to assert one's ethnic identity. The university could be transformed from a potential threat to identity into an instru-

mentality through which to find a new wholeness—an instrumentality potentially more effective than church, family, and community.

For those black students, references in reading assignments or lectures that tended to enhance blacks' sense of identity and self-worth seemed few and far between. In the liberal arts, blacks (and practically all other nonwhites) scarcely existed. In American history, blacks were viewed as slaves or as problems, rarely as contributing anything of value, or even as being central, to the American experience. Black authors were seldom included in courses in American literature; such black characters as occurred in "white" fiction, like Twain's Nigger Jim and Faulkner's Dilsey, often raised difficult questions about black identity. Social science, with its pose of objectivity, was perhaps most painful of all to black students, who complained that blacks were viewed by most sociologists, economists, and political scientists as deviants from a norm arbitrarily defined by white social scientists.

The solution, as many blacks saw it, was courses in African history and civilization, Afro-American history, Afro-American literature, Afro-American "culture," or Afro-American contributions to American "culture." But most white faculty members knew next to nothing about those topics, and were inclined, not surprisingly, to regard what they did not know about—what none of their colleagues ever talked or wrote about—as being of little or no importance. Few scholars were sympathetic, most were condescending, and some were actively hostile to the suggestion that the black experience in any of its manifestations was worthy of study. Many were heard to comment that the very idea of *black* economics, *black* sociology, or *black* literature was ludicrous. All of which is to say that the problem implicit in the student complaint—the blind ethnocentrism of American higher education—was for the most part ignored.

A major obstacle for those who wanted courses for identity building was that this was not what most scholars understood their function to be. Courses in history explicitly intended to identify and venerate heroes and heroines, to celebrate a people's "contribution," to make students feel good about themselves did not command the respect of good scholars. History had a different—a critical and analytical—role to play. Of what good was a literature course taught and attended by people so in awe of the mere existence of certain works that there was little room for criticism and textual analysis? Most teachers were likely to say "You can read anytime; courses are to make you think in a disciplined way." The onus was on Afro-American studies to prove that it did just that.

Students in search of their ethnic and personal identity did not automatically seek separatist solutions, although the hostility or indifference of faculty members tended to move them in that direction. These students generally believed that there was no intrinsic reason to deny Afro-American studies recognition as a bona fide academic discipline. They felt that the major obstacle to Afro-American studies was faculty members who did not take it seriously. The real problem, however, was the students' uncritical acceptance of courses that celebrated the Afro-American past and their hostility to faculty (black more so than white) who insisted on a critical analysis that showed heroes and heroines to be merely human.[27]

A Field of Study

Apart from the need to define an academic turf in a sea of Eurocentric whiteness, and beyond the psychological rationale arguing that courses in history and literature and culture would lead to a healthy discovery of "self," there was the claim that the African/Afro-American experience and culture provided subject matter of legitimate academic study in its own right. The African diaspora, the black presence in the Western Hemisphere and particularly in the United States, provided, it was argued, a historical reality worthy of study for its own sake as well as for its value in understanding conventional history. Afro-American writers had left a literature, there was an Afro-American musical heritage, and there was folklore, none of which had received adequate academic attention. Courses should be offered in Afro-American studies to fill a gap in scholarship and to spur scholarly interest in a neglected field.

By the sixties, actual scholarship in what was to be called Afro-American studies had a considerable history. The names of W.E.B. DuBois, Carter G. Woodson, and Arthur Schomburg, whose works date back to the first decade of the twentieth century, are well enough known to illustrate this point. There were others like them whose names are not so well known. Aside from their personal scholarship, they joined with others in support of such scholarly organizations as the American Negro Academy (1897-1915) and Woodson's Association for the Study of Negro Life and History, which was established in 1916 and which is now called the Association for the Study of Afro-American Life and History.

This early generation established a tradition of careful and conventional scholarship. Their work, however, was largely unacknowledged by professional historians. Except for a small group of blacks (academics in southern schools and amateurs) and a smaller number of whites, there was little interest in Afro-American life and history. By the fifties one might have identified a subfield of American history called "Negro history," but that was something taught almost exclusively in black schools. Less could be said for Afro-American literature. Articles on Negro history could not be found in the two major historical journals—*The American Historical Review* and the *Mississippi Valley Historical Review*—unless they could pass as "southern history." As a consequence, the *Journal of Negro History* (Carter Woodson's creation) had its pick of the very best scholarly work being done.

The white scholarly establishment was not hospitable. There was a predisposition among historians, for instance, to believe that blacks could not be objective about their history, especially since their interpretations were likely to run counter to conventional wisdom.[28] The onus was on the black scholar to prove himself or herself unbiased; ideally such scholars would produce scholarship that disguised the fact that the authors were black. Only whites could be presumed unbiased. In the effort to gain professional respectability, black scholars were likely to try to make themselves color-blind in their work.

Despite efforts at conformity, such scholars as DuBois, Woodson, Rayford Logan, and Benjamin Quarles were aware of the entrenched racism in their profession. They were of a "progressive" generation, however, and imagined that reason and demonstrated quality would in time be recognized. Meanwhile, something should be done to educate Afro-American young people to understand and appreciate their past, to see themselves not only through the eyes of white American scholars whose interpretations of slavery, Reconstruction, and the historical oppression of blacks were by no means disinterested. That was much of the reason behind the establishment of the American Negro Academy and the Association for the Study of Negro Life and History, that is, the creation and dissemination of a useable past for black Americans. Carter Woodson railed against what he called "the mis-education of the Negro," arguing that conventional schooling in America (the North as well as the South) brainwashed blacks into a belief in the superiority of whites and in blacks' lack of history or culture. To correct that, one needed scholarship. DuBois, too, came to argue the special responsibility of southern black colleges to support such scholarship for the purpose of teaching black youth who, otherwise, would be mis-educated.[29] All of these men, however, called for the soundest scholarship.

In the sixties, the few black Ph.D.'s were likely to echo these beliefs. They were prepared to support Afro-American history courses, willing to advocate their scholarly importance, but insistent on professional standards of scholarship. In the last regard they differed with student advocates of such programs. This older generation of scholars tended also to be distrustful of (or ambivalent about) the students' efforts to politicize the program, to make an academic program the instrument of ideology.

37

They preferred to see such courses taught within conventional departments, for two reasons: (1) the department would give a legitimacy and stability to something new to the institution; and (2) such courses would be a foothold, a beginning, in the reform of the scholarly profession. As we will see, these expectations ran counter to what students and some of their faculty allies wanted.

I have written here mainly of historians, in part because they were asked to play a major role in Afro-American studies. (To the extent that there was a field, it depended on them.) Sociology, perhaps, had the largest number of black scholars interested in the Afro-American. Race relations had, from the 1890s, been a recognized academic field, one in which both white and black scholars had built reputations. Beginning with the work of Robert Park, the University of Chicago had been a center of this study, supporting such scholars as Eric Reuter, E. Franklin Frazier, Horace Cayton, and St. Clair Drake. Black sociologists like Charles S. Johnson, Ira De A. Reid, Frazier, Cayton, and Drake had built national reputations. But sociology as a field was not ready to supply leadership to Afro-American studies.

In the first place, most of the old scholarship (whether by blacks or whites) seemed to view its black subjects pathologically, with whites as the exemplary norm. Furthermore, the field of sociology was beginning to splinter. The newer, positivistic, quantifying scholarship was becoming predominant in the field (as it was in other social sciences), and such qualitative and relatively subjective topics as race relations were receiving less respect. The profession began to split over methodology and, as the sixties advanced, it split racially as well. Black sociologists created separate caucuses to establish an independent direction and to criticize what they began to refer to as "white sociology."[30] The deep racial and ideological divisions within sociology were perhaps best illustrated by the rancor and division generated by the so-called Moynihan Report.

It is important to observe that the black sociologists

who took the lead as advocates of Afro-American studies were likely to be at the radical edge in this split. Both Nathan Hare and Harry Edwards were deeply cynical about, and distrustful of, institutions and traditional academic fields. Their tendency was to be anti-intellectual and anti-"Establishment." Edwards saw the black student movement as providing the "impetus for violent and irreversible revolution in America." And he saw the object of black leadership and black studies as being to "fight the mainstream to establish black authenticity and to achieve full equality or be overwhelmed in the attempt."[31] It should be said, however, that St. Clair Drake, a senior and respected scholar, early took on the direction of Afro-American studies at Stanford and made it one of the best programs in the country.

The humanities (excluding history) were always the most Eurocentric of American scholarly fields. English literature, philosophy, art history, and music were, in the sixties, the fields least touched by subject matter having to do with black Americans. Of these fields, literature, music, and the fine arts had the least excuse; American literature was a field where blacks had played a role. It was a rare college course in a northern school that taught any black author—until Ralph Ellison and James Baldwin became fashionable. There were, however, a number of senior black scholars in American literature: J. Saunders Redding, Blyden Jackson, Charles Davis, George Kent, to name a few. Most taught in southern black colleges. Professionally, the modern languages are so factionalized that it was almost natural for scholars of black literature to become merely another faction within the professional ranks. As activity in the subject developed, room was made for them, as it would be made, for example, for Chicano literature. Very little room would be made, however, in the canon of American literature or in the mainstream curriculum.

Those who wanted Afro-American studies to be recognized as an academic discipline generally held that it should emphasize three existing academic fields: history, literature, and sociology—especially history.[32] Once one confronted the problem of getting scholars to take Afro-American studies seriously, one also had the task of explaining how such disparate fields could be brought together in it. Those who took the matter most seriously were the most uncomfortable with the character of student demands. As scholar-teachers, they saw their object as being the development of a teaching field that would remain academically respectable to their peers, and they saw as the primary object of any course the giving of an academic competence to students. Those aims could be hostile to demands for a program as a quest for power or personal (racial) identity. These conflicts would plague the supporters of Afro-American studies throughout the seventies.

Three basic concerns lay behind the demand for Afro-American studies—the political need for turf and place, the psychological need for identity, and the academic need for recognition. While they might be discussed as separate questions for the sake of convenience, they were really inseparable. Individuals could be driven by more than one of these needs. As long as matters remained at the reform stage, implicit differences could be ignored. When it came time to build and define programs, compatibility among the various agents of reform became strained. Scholars who once found the "student constituent" useful in establishing the urgency of the program might well find that student views of an academic program did not comport well with their own. Students who had hoped to find psychological and emotional support in new courses might find them both academically difficult and emotionally troubling. Once the programs were in place—the need for "turf" having been achieved—black students might not even take the courses, or might act as though taking them were a political statement rather than an academic choice. Furthermore, there came in the mid-seventies a generation of students—both black and white—who were highly career-oriented. Courses that existed largely to make rhetorical and political stat-
40

ments had little appeal to students whose main concern was admission to a professional school. By 1975, the decade of ideology was over

PATTERNS OF IDEOLOGY
The black student movement, in sharp contrast to the white, was virtually indifferent to Marxist ideology. Doctrinal disputes within the American Left over Marxism had been intense since World War I, and what conflict there was within the white-student left can be seen as a continuation of the tradition.

Most blacks, if asked, would have defined themselves as sympathetic to the Marxian interpretation of social change (that is, to the view that racial oppression was the result of an exploitative economic system) and to the view that racial justice would most likely be achieved under some form of socialism, but few were committed to an ideological faction. (Angela Davis, of course, had been an exception.) They would have said, rather, that their unity in blackness transcended political factionalism.

They divided themselves roughly into two camps: integrationists and separatists. This division had to do not so much with desired goals for a future society as with a predisposition to work with whites in conventional institutions or to focus on self-development among blacks. The one was not necessarily antiblack, nor the other necessarily antiwhite; they had, rather, to do with efficacy and the relative importance one placed on racial identification. The separatists, also, could be divided into "black power" advocates and cultural nationalists.

Integrationists
Few in this group defended American colleges' and universities' past or present policies with regard to race. Few denied the need for courses having to do with Afro-Americans. Hardly any found white faculty and administrators faultless in their attitudes and feelings about race. Integrationists, however, insisted that blacks had to succeed in terms of these imperfect institutions and people,

41

the better to function in the even less perfect world outside. Nothing could be gained, save the comforts of self-
indulgence, by defining oneself outside the system. Black
students and their faculty allies, the integrationists felt,
made a serious mistake in demanding an "autonomy"
that would only result in the creation of an academic
ghetto, providing an excuse for whites to dismiss blacks
as irrelevant or to treat them with patronizing condescension.

The institution, the integrationists felt, was important
to blacks for the skills training it offered—skills blacks
had been denied. It was important also for the experience
it offered blacks in management—the management of
white peers and of an institutional bureaucracy as complicated and sophisticated as that of a university. Finally,
the institution was a certifying agency whose graduates
were assumed to possess intelligence, competence, and
discipline, qualities essential to professional training and
employment. To the integrationist, separating oneself
from the institution or undermining it was self-defeating.
Not only must one work through the institution, but one
should protect its academic integrity while getting it to
adopt Afro-American programs. Any victory would be
hollow if its "spoils" were debased in the process of being
won. Integrationists, therefore, were seen as defenders of
the university and were often attacked by student radi-
cals as having been co-opted.

Of course, integrationists were hostile to student
demands for separate facilities. They preferred to see
black studies courses offered in the standard curriculum,
in conventional departments; perhaps, like other interdisciplinary programs, administered by a committee
made up of faculty from the several departments
involved. They were suspicious that an argument for
"autonomy" was really a plea for racially separate (and
black-controlled) programs. While they might concede
that blacks, because of special experience, would bring
a unique and necessary perspective to courses in black
studies, they rejected the idea that such courses should
42

be taught only by blacks and could not be well taught by whites. While they advocated the increased hiring of black faculty (whether or not they supported affirmative action programs), they did not want to see black faculty strictly tied to black studies, or affirmative action goals met by the packing of blacks into black studies programs. They were likely to urge white faculty to teach courses in the program.

Integrationists were the least troubled by alienation from the black community as they did not see success in the university and professional life as a rejection of black people. They were, as a result, unlikely to support demands for "community programs" except in such service roles as tutoring in the schools or churches. And they were ambivalent in their relations with black student groups. The integrationist black student preferred to be independent (to have white as well as black friends, for instance), but in the sixties and seventies that role was difficult.

Separatists—"Black Power"
The "black power" rhetoric of Stokely Carmichael in 1966 signaled an ideological shift among blacks generally and the student movement in particular. The new position argued that blacks, by conforming to the demands of white institutions, white liberals, and even white allies and supporters, were allowing values and strategies to be defined by white people, the most well-meaning of whom were ignorant of, or indifferent to, genuine black needs. More important, whites were hostile to the thought of power being in the hands of black people. They would give blacks everything except what they needed: power and the self-respect that comes with it. By making alliances with whites—by allowing them to define issues, strategies, and goals—blacks were denying themselves the responsibilities of leadership and community building. Furthermore, blacks in these alliances were being co-opted and removed from their real source of strength, their natural constituency: black people. Finally, white

43

allies would abandon blacks whenever it served their interest to do so.

The "black power" argument was, therefore, one of self-reliance. It was separatist because it saw community building and race consciousness as essential first steps in the achievement of a program. Black people had to become self-reliant economically and politically before they could bring genuine power into play; without power they would always be dependent. Once they had power, however, coalitions with whites and others would not only be possible and desirable but effective. In this sense, then, theirs was not an absolutist, separatist strategy. It was more of a tactic intended to lead to a more fruitful interracial cooperation.

The demands for "autonomous" black studies programs must be seen in light of this "black power" ideology. At bottom, autonomy was a question of power. Would the university give to blacks (students included) the power imagined to exist in a department or college? In some ways, the answer to this question was more important to those making the demand than was the substance of the program or the efficacy of such "autonomous" agencies in achieving academic objectives. "Black power" also informed the demand for black dormitories, student centers, and the like. Community building implied the coming together of black people on and off campus as a community. In this regard, it is important to observe that these students were unknown to one another before coming to college and were often from places that, at best, were disintegrating communities. They were the more anxious, therefore, to tie themselves to the local black community as a defense against the perceived co-opting pressures of the institution.

On the positive side, "black power" proponents claimed that blacks had the ability and the obligation to create their own world on their own terms (just as whites had done). On the negative side, "black power" was an attitude deliberately inhospitable to whites. One wanted blacks on the faculty, of course, but especially to teach

44

courses in Afro-American studies. Black faculty would have a perspective different from whites. More important, the appointment of black faculty and the control of the Afro-American studies program by blacks would be a delivery of power into black hands. Some argued that whites had nothing of value to say about blacks and that the program should be controlled by blacks without interference from white faculty and administration.

Some programs—notably at the University of Illinois at Chicago Circle and at Cornell—kept a strong "black power" orientation. Since the decline of interest in black studies in the mid-seventies, supporters have seldom talked of autonomy, turning, rather, to guarantees of continued university support. Most of those that started with separatist notions either expired or moderated their positions.

Separatism—Cultural Nationalism
This aspect of separatist ideology was of slight real influence on college campuses but should be mentioned to distinguish it from that of "black power." "Black power" advocates believed it possible to negotiate with and otherwise relate to whites on the basis of power; cultural nationalists like Maulana Ron Karenga of UCLA did not. Like the "black power" advocates, Karenga placed great emphasis on community building among blacks, but he went further in assuming two nations and two cultures—one white and one black. Even while attached to the university Karenga was deeply antagonistic to it, especially to its efforts to be helpful to black people. His model was a colonial one: blacks, as he saw it, were emerging from colonial status into nationhood. The university's proper role, he maintained, was (1) "nonintervention" in the black community, with no efforts to influence it or shape it; (2) separation—as an institution of the former colonizing power, the university should deliver financial and technical aid but only as black people demanded it; and (3) the creation of a movement to civilize white people. While such notions were not cen-

45

tral to black student thought, they did inform some of the rhetoric.[33] As we shall see, such ideological presuppositions defined the form as well as the style the new programs took.

TYPICAL MODELS
The models on which Afro-American studies programs were built were influenced by ideology and conditions on individual campuses. Naturally, each particular form had intrinsic strengths and weaknesses.

The Program
From an academic point of view, the "program" approach has been the most successful. It acknowledges the interdisciplinary character of Afro-American studies by using faculty from established departments. It relies on the president and the dean to guarantee the program through budget allocations to the departments involved. While a faculty member's appointment may be principally to offer courses and service to Afro-American studies, his or her membership remains within the department of discipline. By definition, all senior faculty in a program are jointly appointed to a department and to the program. Because of this structure, it is relatively easy for the program to exploit the curricula of other departments; it is not necessary for the program to provide all of the courses its students are expected to take.

Most Afro-American studies offerings in the country follow the program model. A good example is the Yale program. Its success had much to do with the willingness of student advocates to accept this plan rather than insist on "autonomy." It has been noted for the broad range of faculty involvement. Names like Sidney Mintz, Charles Davis, Robert Thompson, and John Blassingame have been associated with it. Davis, until his recent death, served as director; his place has been taken by Blassingame. Young scholars of remarkably high quality have been in the program—especially in literature. Names like

46

Robert Stepto, Henry Gates, and Houston Baker come to mind. Apparently from the beginning, association with the program has been judged with approval in academic circles. The Yale program is one of the few in the country offering a graduate program leading to a master's degree.

The strengths of this model are obvious, but principally they reside in its capacity to engage a wide range of departments and faculty in the service of Afro-American studies. This, of course, would not have been a strength to those of markedly separatist persuasion. Its major weakness, as those who argued for autonomy predicted, is its dependence for survival on the continued support and good will of others in the university: the president, dean, and the heads of cooperating departments, among others. Yale's program has not been troubled in this regard, but other programs have, especially when enrollments drop or when there is disagreement about standards or goals.

Programs like Yale's are designed to offer undergraduates a major (or field of concentration) for their degree. Not all programs do. Some merely offer a few courses with a focus on subject matter having to do with Afro-American life. Such courses may be accepted for credit by the student's major department (for example, economics) or may serve merely as an elective. Wesleyan, for instance, until recently had a complicated system in which an Afro-American studies major was possible but in which students found it difficult to put the necessary courses together; they thus majored elsewhere and took the one or two Afro-American studies courses as electives. (The Wesleyan program has undergone changes designed to strengthen and improve it.) The program at the University of Rhode Island is also of interest in this regard. It offers special courses: one, for example, on free-enterprise zones, and another on human resources. Such courses are designed to serve students interested in working in the community or in Third World countries. These courses do not lead to a degree in Afro-American studies, but they serve students in special programs such as a master's program in international development.

The College

The most radical kind of Afro-American studies program was that of the independent college—sometimes an all-black college—within the university. That was the demand at San Francisco State and at Cornell. The ethnic studies department at Berkeley, existing outside the College of Arts and Sciences, had for a while something of a de facto college status. Afro-American studies, however, defected and became a standing department in Arts and Sciences in 1974. No other major university came close to acceding to this extreme demand.

Local community colleges sometimes became de facto all-black colleges. That was surely the case with Malcolm X College in Chicago. It is a community college, supported by public funds, but located in an area almost wholly black. Formerly Crane Junior College, it became Malcolm X in 1968 when it moved to its present location. Its student population is about 80 percent black, 8 percent Hispanic, and 12 percent other. While it offers a range of black-oriented courses, it specializes in computer sciences and health services. Whether or not it was planned to be so, circumstance permits it to be the kind of college the separatists demanded. It is difficult to know how many other such community colleges there are.

The Department

The more practical model for those who insisted on autonomy was the department. A department had its own budget, could appoint and dismiss its own faculty and staff, design its own curriculum, and service its student concentrators without any control or oversight by others. It was also assumed to be a more permanent structure than a program. Some institutions established Afro-American studies departments without much ado. In others, like Harvard, departmental status remained a bone of contention years after it was established. The more it was resisted, of course, the more it appeared to be worth fighting for and defending.

The argument against it was mainly that a department

48

normally represented a discipline. Afro-American studies, being interdisciplinary in character, should, critics said, be organized into a program made up of faculty from the various departments serving it. Its defenders most often claimed it was a discipline defined by its particular perspective on a topic none of the other departments offered. In these terms the argument was tendentious. As defined by the nineteenth-century German university, departments were identical with academic disciplines. By 1969, however, that had ceased to be true of American university departments. Interdisciplinary departments had developed within the sciences, and occasionally area studies were departmentally organized. On the other hand, a perspective, which was what Afro-American studies offered, could hardly be thought of as a discipline. Whatever it once was, a department is now largely an administrative convenience. Afro-American studies departments have worked reasonably well in some institutions, Berkeley and the University of Indiana being examples. It did not work well at Harvard, and its problems illuminate some of the weaknesses of the model.

Departmental autonomy, it turns out, is not as absolute as some believed. Such autonomy as exists carries problems. Under a program, the president and dean can, in effect, direct departments to make searches and appoint competent faculty approved by the program's committee. The department has the power and budget to make recommendations for appointment, but, lacking other arrangements, it must find scholars willing to take positions in Afro-American studies alone. In practice, most senior scholars with major reputations insist on joint appointments with the departments of their discipline. So, most often, an Afro-American studies department's appointment is contingent on another department's approval of its candidate. Such arrangements presuppose good will and respect among the departments involved. In such ways, autonomy can work against the department's efforts. Furthermore, even when university

49

budgets were more ample, it was impossible for an Afro-American studies department to provide faculty in all of the disciplines thought useful to it. As a result, they are forced to depend on a very limited program (history and literature) or rely on other departments' offerings.

Whatever the expectation of those who struggled to create departments rather than programs, joint appointments are the general rule throughout the country. Sometimes this resulted from administrative fiat, sometimes out of necessity. Ewart Guinier, the first chairman of Harvard's department, had no joint appointment himself and attempted to make the question of departmental autonomy and integrity rest on the power to promote a junior person to tenure from within. The president and the dean, responding to university-wide criticism of the department's program and standards, in 1974 made promotion from within the Afro-American studies department conditional upon joint appointment. Guinier failed in his effort to force this issue in his favor. This case illustrates another important limit to departmental autonomy. Appointment and tenure matters must be concurred in by university-wide and ad hoc committees (in Harvard's case these committees are made up of outside scholars appointed by the dean), and, finally, only the president makes appointments.

The practice of joint appointments is a good thing when it works well. It dispels suspicion about the quality of a department's faculty, especially necessary in a new field in which standards and reputation are in question. Furthermore, it gives Afro-American studies a voice and an advocate within the conventional departments, which is quite useful for communication and good will. In this regard, the practice achieves some of the good features of programs. Whether imposed by the administration or adopted as a matter of convenience, however, joint appointments may be the cause of problems and friction. A candidate may fail to win tenure in the second department, its faculty claiming a failure to meet their standards. Since questions of standards are seldom easy to resolve, these decisions are likely to cause antagonism and ill will. Joint appointments also raise questions of service, loyalty, and commitment of faculty to Afro-American studies. Once appointed, a faculty member may find it more congenial working in the field of his discipline; if he is tenured, little can be done. From the faculty member's point of view, moreover, joint appointments can pose problems. It is time-consuming to be a good citizen in two departments. Junior faculty, particularly, are likely to feel themselves to be serving two masters, each having its own expectations.

Graduate Programs

Few black studies departments or programs offer work toward a graduate degree. Yale, as has been noted, offers an M.A. in Afro-American studies, which seems to attract student teachers and those who expect to be able to use knowledge thus acquired in community or public service work. The University of Rhode Island offers courses that supplement other master's programs in, for example, human resources and international development. UCLA has a graduate and postdoctoral program and provides no formal undergraduate offering.

The small number of graduate programs is not difficult to understand. Graduate programs in the humanities and social sciences have been shrinking everywhere; some have ceased to exist. Student interest has shifted from academic careers to law, medicine, and business. Furthermore, those who wish to follow scholarly careers are better off working in conventional departments; in universities where they exist, such study could be directed by scholars of Afro-American life. One advantage of this arrangement is that it can help to stimulate scholarship about Afro-Americans in conventional disciplines. In general, however, Afro-American studies faculty lack the advantages that come from having graduate students.

The Undergraduate Center

Sometimes, when there is neither a department nor a program of Afro-American studies, there will be a center, as, for example, the Center for Afro-American Studies at Wesleyan. Such centers have little or no academic program. Mainly, they provide such services to undergraduates as counseling and career guidance. (As at Wesleyan, those services are also available elsewhere in the institution for all students, blacks included.) These centers sponsor programs of interest to black students, are a focal point for extracurricular activities, and are, in effect, black student unions. The existence of such centers reflects the continued sense of exclusion among some black students from such general student activities as campus newspaper, dramatics, and literary magazines, the sense that the typical campus lecture or program has little to say to them and that they must maintain "turf" that is clearly theirs. In places where student-community programs exist, these centers often serve to coordinate them. If Wesleyan is the rule, the existence of such centers is likely to result in a weak academic program and student indifference to that weakness.[34]

The Research Center or Institute

Institutes have long been a means to encourage and support advanced scholarship in the social sciences and, to a lesser degree, in the humanities. While some are unattached to a university, most major universities have been eager to house such centers because they are a source of prestige and serve as inducements to the best and most productive scholars, who, by means of the institute, can pursue advanced studies among colleagues of kindred interests and talents while sheltered to some extent from teaching obligations. Since examples of successful institutes abound, it is little wonder that persons interested in Afro-American studies would attempt their own. The results have been mixed, at best.[35]

Columbia University, with funds from the Ford Foundation, established the Urban Center in 1968–69. Because none of the funds were invested as endowment, and because the university interpreted the terms of the grant as permitting their use for related projects and programs, the Urban Center had either to seek other funding or to expire when the Ford money ran out. Its first director, Franklyn Williams, served only a short time before taking a position at the Phelps-Stokes Fund. The bulk of the original grant went for staff salaries and university overhead. Except for some community-related programs that were federally funded, the Urban Center did very little. Nothing of an academic or scholarly character was developed in the center, and few of the university's faculty were involved. The funds ran out in 1977, and the center was allowed to expire.

The Institute of the Black World (IBW) was established in Atlanta in 1969. It was originally intended to be part of the Martin Luther King, Jr., Memorial Center and to work in cooperation with the Atlanta University Graduate Center, but in the summer of 1970, for ideological and other reasons, IBW split with the King Center and Atlanta University. The King Center came to focus almost entirely on King's literary and ideological legacy, and its leadership was far more integrationist in its approach than the leadership of the IBW.

From the beginning the IBW attracted many of the most capable among those who followed the "black power" mode. Vincent Harding, William Strickland, Howard Dodson, Lerone Bennett, St. Clair Drake, and Sylvia Wynter were among its original board of directors. Claiming to be a "gathering of black scholar/activists," it remained consistently intellectual and serious in scholarly intent.[36]

IBW's funding came from a variety of sources. In 1969–70, perhaps its most promising year, it received grants from Wesleyan University, the Ford Foundation, the Cummins Engine Foundation, and the Southern Education Foundation. The level of funding was far lower over the next decade, yet the institute managed to generate position papers from scholars and others that were generally of good quality and provocative. In 1983, with its staff much reduced and its principal office now in Washington, D.C.,

53

IBW, it is fair to say, has ceased to function as a center for scholarly research. It is now seeking funds for a major film that will provide a black perspective on American history.

The W.E.B. DuBois Institute for Afro-American Studies was established at Harvard in 1975 by President Derek Bok. Seen perhaps as a corrective to Harvard's highly political, radical, and contentious Afro-American studies department, the DuBois Institute was designed for advanced study of Afro-American life, history, and culture. During its first five years, led by a series of "acting directors," the institute supported lectures and other programs, but mainly offered predoctoral fellowships to four or five advanced graduate students a year. The object of the predoctoral program was to identify promising graduate students and to support them through the successful completion of their dissertations. Funding for that program (from the Henry R. Luce Foundation) ran out in 1981. Funds for the balance of the institute's program were provided by the university.

In the past three years, the institute has sponsored major art exhibits, lectures, and concerts. With funds from the Ford Foundation, it has inaugurated an annual lecture series and, since 1983–84, it has supported in residence two senior scholars a year. It has appointed four postdoctoral research fellows each year since 1980–81. Proposals are now being designed for multiyear research projects on criminal justice, economics and public policy, public health, and education. The intention is that the DuBois Institute will generate major research projects on questions and problems related to Afro-American life and experience, sustaining a broad range of scholarship.

The Carter G. Woodson Institute for Afro-American and African Studies was established by the University of Virginia in 1981 with a mandate to encourage research and teaching in all the geographic components of the black experience: the African, Afro-Latin, Afro-Caribbean, and Afro-American. Funded by the Ford Foundation, the institute supervises the university's undergraduate Afro-American and African Studies Program; sponsors colloquia,
54

lectures, and conferences; and others both pre- and post-doctoral fellowships in the humanities and social sciences for research and writing in black studies.

At UCLA, the Afro-American Studies Program is a quasi-institute in form. It supports research by graduate students and postdoctoral scholars. This program offers no instructional courses.

The research institute seems the most attractive and useful instrument to develop serious scholarship in this field. So far, none have succeeded in establishing themselves. There are several reasons: (1) there are too few high-quality scholars in the field to support several competing centers; (2) ideology has tended to dominate some, weakening their appeal to some of the best scholars; (3) lack of capital funding has forced them all to rely on funds generated year by year and on the generosity of a host institution. Furthermore, most university-based institutions can rely on university faculty to generate their own funds, which then can be funneled through the appropriate institute. Scholarship on Afro-American topics is in no university general enough to offer much help in this way. Afro-American institutes' directors and program officers must both generate their own programs and discover the scholars to do the work.

VARIETIES OF CURRICULUM
A continuing debate rages as to whether Afro-American studies is a legitimate discipline. Many in the black studies movement have taken this question very seriously and have attempted to define the discipline in a core curriculum. The National Council for Black Studies, in a 1981 report, defined the purpose and rationale of such a program: (1) to provide skills; (2) to provide a standard and purposefully direct student choice; (3) to achieve "liberation of the black community"; (4) to enhance self-awareness and esteem. Black studies, the report says, "inaugurates an unflinching attack on institutional oppression/racism." It also aims to question "the ade-

55

quacy, objectivity and universal scope of other schools of thought; it assumes a critical posture."[37]

The National Council apparently understood discipline to mean doctrine, for it goes on to outline in detail a course of study that would cover the four undergraduate years. It would begin in the African past and end in the American present, touching on the nonblack world only to show racism and its oppressive consequences. If students following this program were to take courses in the sciences, or acquire any of the specific analytical skills associated with the social sciences, they would have to take them as electives. There have been other efforts to design a core curriculum in Afro-American studies, for example, at the University of Illinois—Chicago Circle. Such efforts are notable for their attempt to create an undergraduate curriculum totally independent of other departments and offerings.

Limited budgets and the interdisciplinary nature of most Afro-American studies programs make it impossible to staff such a program as the National Council recommends. For the most part, existing programs stress Afro-American history and culture. That stands to reason, because the great teaching opportunities have been in this area. Afro-American history and literature are fairly well-developed fields, and there has been a notable black production in music and the arts. It has been harder to create good courses in the social sciences (or to appoint good scholars, for that matter). That is because, except for sociology, none of the social sciences have taken subject matter and problems related to black Americans to be of such importance in their disciplines as to constitute a specialization. Few economists or political scientists are willing to define themselves as specialists on Afro-American questions.

The recent shift in student interests to business and law, and the universal interest (especially among funding sources) in public policy is pushing Afro-American studies programs to emphasize the social sciences more than they have. I suspect, also, that the growing preoccupation among social scientists with public policy will push them into more questions having to do with blacks, and they may find it to their advantage to be associated with an Afro-American studies department. Courses on the economics of discrimination, urban politics, social mobility, and the like are logical offerings in an Afro-American studies department.

A word should be said about typical courses in the humanities. Except for those in literature, the tendency of Afro-American programs is to offer courses in the performing arts rather than their scholarly counterparts. Art courses are seldom art history; music is taught rather than musicology and music history; and there are courses in dance. This is important to note because it varies from the traditional liberal arts relegation of performing arts to extracurricular activities.

Afro-American studies programs remain tailored to available talent and other institutional resources. For the most part, they are based on some combination of history and literature with enough additional courses to fill out an undergraduate major. Many closely resemble such interdisciplinary programs as American studies. In practice, however, few students choose to major in Afro-American studies, preferring to select Afro-American studies courses as electives or, when possible, as course credit toward a conventional major in, for example, history. At the University of Illinois at Urbana/Champaign, for instance, the majority of course offerings in Afro-American subjects are in other departments, Afro-American studies acting as a service department. Harvard has attempted in the past four years to design an undergraduate concentration similar to other interdisciplinary programs in the college, namely history and literature and social studies. Beginning with a base in Afro-American history and literature, the student is directed through tutorials and selected courses toward achieving an academic competence in more than one discipline. Harvard also permits joint concentrations in the college, so it becomes possible for students to link Afro-American studies with one of the other departments. This has become a popular option. At Harvard, as elsewhere, the current preprofessional emphasis among undergraduates makes many wary of a major which they think might jeopardize admission to a professional school.[38]

After the initial demand for Afro-American studies courses, there followed a rather sharp decline in interest. The peak years were 1968 through 1970. By 1974, there was general concern that these programs would become extinct for lack of enrollment. The reasons for the decline in student interest were many: (1) students, both black and white, increasingly turned from political to career concerns; (2) the atmosphere in many courses was hostile and antagonistic to white students; (3) many of the courses lacked substance and academic rigor; and (4) campus communities had been exhausted by the rhetoric, bombast, and revolutionary ideology that still permeated many of these courses and programs. The white guilt many black activists had relied on had been spent.[39] Born, as these programs were, out of campus crises, in an era of highly charged rhetoric, unconditional demands, and cries for revolution, it was difficult for them to shake that style and reputation.

INSTITUTIONAL CONTEXT

The programs that survived naturally reflected the circumstances in which they were created. In the short run, colleges like Yale and Stanford, where programs were adopted in relative calm, seem to be among the soundest and most stable. Furthermore, those that opted for programs—avoiding faculty conflict over departmental status—have tended to enjoy the easiest relationship in their academic communities. For the others, the legacy of conflict and bickering about status and legitimacy have continued to be troublesome. Evaluations and judgments about every program must therefore be made in the context of its particular college and history. At schools like Berkeley, Cornell, Columbia, and Harvard, the events of 1968 through 1970 deeply divided the faculty; bitterness stemming from those divisions remains, though muted and controlled. Issues and problems related to Afro-American studies continue to provoke emotional rather than reasoned responses. In most places, however, the programs are accepted as "here to stay," so both hostility and anxiety tend to be more latent than overt.[40]

The history of the efforts to establish Afro-American studies makes us aware of how deeply conservative faculties are. Change is usually very slow in academic institutions, and most conflict is resolved by consensus. In this sense, Afro-American studies was a shock to the system. In the past, new departments (biochemistry, for instance) were created only after years of development within established disciplines; the production of scholarship and fresh knowledge was antecedent to, and justification for, the new department. Even so, there was friction and dissent. It was many years before English departments acknowledged the importance of American literature, and many advocates of the establishment of American studies programs (or departments) have failed to overcome resistance to what some see as their novelty. Little wonder that Afro-American studies had a chilly reception. Many scholars—some out of ignorance and bigotry, others out of healthy skepticism—wondered whether there was enough there to make a field of study. Many have yet to be convinced. Those scholars of Afro-American life, history, and culture who are careless of and indifferent to the opinions of whites and blacks outside their fields will not convince many skeptics. Others, however, are successfully influencing the scholarly community. Most often, they are based in the more viable Afro-American studies programs and, to my mind, constitute the strongest argument for such programs.

With falling enrollments and the budget crunch, there has been considerable anxiety that Afro-American programs will lose support within the university. Anxiety has been increased by the fact that most such programs were, in some sense, created in response to the political demands of a constituency that, since the mid-seventies, has largely ceased to exist. Many black students abandoned these courses because they lacked academic substance. Criticism previously ignored was taken seriously, and the most egregious courses and behavior were excised.

Student enrollments leveled off after 1974. They will probably never again approach the level of 1970, but they seem, at the moment, to be low (in most places) or modest, but stable.[41] Despite the fears (or hopes) that they would be allowed to die, few programs have done so. The fact that they have remained part of the academic landscape is likely to encourage more constructive relationships with other parts of the university. For political as well as demographic reasons, most state institutions are not likely to discontinue support, even in the face of serious budget constraints. The University of Michigan has been forced to eliminate some departments. Geography has been forced out, but Afro-American studies has not been touched so far. The fact is that some departments and programs—those at Berkeley, Harvard, and Wesleyan, for example—are becoming stronger in program and in character of enrollment.[42]

Even with the passing of generations of students, some of the problems that provoked unrest among black students in the sixties persist. The conservative national trends reflected in white student attitudes are making some black students feel even more isolated than before. The former liberal consensus is no longer present to lend support and encouragement to blacks in their struggle for racial justice. Some white faculty and students may be openly hostile to programs like affirmative action and to admissions policies that give preference to blacks and other minorities. Some may challenge their right to take the place of those assumed to have superior records.[43] In recent years there have been racial incidents involving the denigration of blacks at schools like Wesleyan, the University of Cincinnati, the University of California at Santa Barbara, and Dartmouth. Blacks are more likely to experience racial hostility now than they were a decade

60

ago. These trends are offset by fifteen years of a sizable black presence in northern colleges; blacks are more likely to be taken in stride, and less likely to be made to feel exotic.

Many of the problems black students complained of—then and now—are hard to distinguish from the kinds of complaints all students make. The college years are a difficult time of transition for young people. Separation from home and family, acceptance of adult responsibilities, the formation of new friendships and the loss of old ones, the challenging of one's loyalties to family, class, and community, are problems everyone faces in these years. In the more prestigious colleges, individuals who had always been at the top in their classes in high school may suddenly find that they are unremarkable, even mediocre, in the new setting. These problems, common as they are, have a special impact on black students, who may view them as a "black experience in a white institution" and seek to interpret as a collective condition what are basically individual and personal problems. As a result, many black students continue to seek "identity" in courses about black people, try to establish or maintain black centers such as Wesleyan's Malcolm X House, and work to effect community outreach programs in the local black community. Insofar as they insist that Afro-American studies programs be the instrumentalities to achieve these ends, those programs will be weakened in their academic purpose and reputation.[44]

One of the principal arguments against the establishment of Afro-American studies was the claim that such programs would have the effect of "ghettoizing" both the field and black academics. By establishing such departments, it was said, the traditional departments would be absolved of responsibility for that subject matter. They could remain as lily-white in attitude and faculty as they had always been, now with the assurance that whatever there was to the subject could be taught in Afro-American studies. It was also feared that the challenge of affirmative action could be met simply in the staffing of such departments. In the context of separatist and "black power" ideology, these fears were the more compelling. The argument was that, ironically, black studies would prevent the broad study of Afro-American life and history in the standard curriculum and offer a way off the hook for faculties and departments reluctant to meet affirmative action criteria.

It is impossible to know with certainty how this problem has been met. It is clear that in colleges following the program model, faculty and courses serving the program are based in departments. This, as I have pointed out, is one of the strengths of that model. Elsewhere it is unclear.

The question, it seems to me, is not whether English departments offer courses in Afro-American literature, but whether works by black authors are taught in courses on American literature. A similar question can be asked of other departments—political science, economics, history, and so forth: do those faculties feel a lesser need to include within their courses matter pertaining to the Afro-American experience because black studies programs exist? I do not know the answer to that question, but my impression is that American history has gone farther in developing Afro-American subject matter than other fields and has been the most affected by recent scholarship. The discussion of black authors in standard English courses remains rare. Except for Ralph Ellison (and sometimes Richard Wright and James Baldwin), black authors are largely ignored. Afro-American literature is taken by most white scholars to be a subfield and taught only by those who specialize in it. It is fair to say, however, that there is a much wider knowledge about a few black authors now than fifteen years ago. While this does not answer the question, it suggests that conventional departments have not leapt into the field; they have been slow and grudging. Yet it cannot be proven that without Afro-American studies they would have done better. The need for integration of this subject matter into mainstream courses is great and should be one of the principal tasks in the years ahead.

I have suggested a tendency to confound Afro-American studies with affirmative action. This is partly owing to the tendency of early reformers to combine them in their package of demands. They called for black studies programs and for more black faculty, sometimes, as we have seen, insisting that only blacks should teach black studies. Black candidates who are eligible for academic positions are very few in all fields. Their scarcity has resulted in resentments: one has to offer more to get them (earlier tenure, higher salaries, etc.), departments are burdened by affirmative action procedures adding to departmental administrative chores, departments have a feeling of undue pressure from those administrators who take affirmative action guidelines seriously.

These attitudes affect Afro-American studies programs in giving the general impression that the only black faculty available are in Afro-American studies. I have found, especially among social scientists, a tendency to believe that the only persons willing (and able) to teach Afro-American studies are black. Some fail to acknowledge the potential relevance of their own courses to the field.

Problems of Black Scholars

Black scholars, scarce enough in the past, will be even scarcer in the coming years, it seems. They have been in great demand, but they are likely to be ambivalent about membership in black studies departments. Their reputations as scholars will have to be made in their scholarly discipline, and they are likely to have to explain to their colleagues their role in such a department. The tumultuous and politicized past of these departments makes it the more difficult and problematic to accept an appointment. An Afro-American studies department has to be strong (or promising) and well located to attract the very best black scholars.

Black faculty complain that they are burdened by work and responsibilities not normally asked of whites. Generally, they are a small minority on any campus (often there

63

are only one or two blacks on a faculty), and black students bring to them all their problems with the institution. Thus, they take on the burden of counseling, negotiating with officials, and peace-keeping. School officials push these burdens on them by placing them on a great number of committees, and calling on them to advise on crises having to do with black students or the local black community. Young faculty get confused signals from the institution: they are seemingly praised and respected for being good and helpful citizens, but promotion and career advancement will depend on scholarship and publications. These are conflicting activities, and black scholars often complain that they do not receive adequate support for research and writing. Undoubtedly they have been partly to blame. Being supportive of black students can be appealing, as can the role of peace-keeper. A sharper and more single-minded commitment to scholarship would help them avoid these traps. But these are not easy choices, especially for the young. In any case, many young black scholars fail to produce much in their early years. And the quality of their scholarship is often disappointing. Frequently, they fail to get tenure and are drawn into administrative positions—if they remain in the academic world at all.

One unfortunate consequence of black studies to Afro-American scholars is that it encourages young scholars to train themselves too narrowly. They become Afro-American historians with little sense of American history—not to mention that of Europe, Africa, or Asia. The same can be said of some black literature scholars.

Student Problems

Afro-American studies presents black students with the special problem of having to sort out the academic, political, and personal significance of this course of study. It can present students with deep conflicts. Departments and programs, as they define themselves, may encourage one or the other of two tendencies: those that become distinctively academic in character will discourage and alienate students searching for identity or desiring to make political statements. Those that serve psychological and political needs will not attract the career-oriented or scholarly student. It will take time for academic programs to establish their natural constituency. That will come, however, as those students interested in careers that address public issues discover that black studies courses are important to their professional training.

A more immediate question for students has to do with how a major in Afro-American studies will affect their chances for admission into graduate and professional schools. Many students and their advisers suspect that admissions committees will not respect an Afro-American studies undergraduate major, but little evidence exists to support that. A good student from a good school will do well regardless of undergraduate major. Graduate training in academic disciplines, however, does require an adequate background in the field the student wishes to follow. With proper foresight, that expectation can easily be met.

One must continue to ask whether particular Afro-American studies programs provide students with a sufficiently broad education and train them to an adequate level of academic competence in a combination of disciplines. Competency in reading and writing is hardly enough to justify a college education. One hopes that students would be helped to develop skills in critical analysis and encouraged in their respect for the intellect— their own as well as others'. Obviously, the critical pose assumed in the National Council for Black Studies' dictum—that it "questions the adequacy, objectivity and universal scope of other schools of thought"—is adequate. One would hope that such programs in Afro-American studies would submit their own programs, pedagogy, and assumptions to as harsh a critical gaze as they level at those of others. The time is past when questions about the rightness or wrongness of Afro-American studies are constructive. Afro-American studies exists and has established itself well enough to continue to exist. Accepting that, it is important to require it to meet standards comparable to those of any other undergraduate major. It should produce students with specific knowledge, and the skills to make use of it, but at the same time a broad enough view of the world and of human experience to place their special knowledge in a meaningful context. It is my impression that very few Afro-American studies programs do this well. There is nothing about the subject matter of the field, or its focus, that makes these criteria impossible.

CONCLUSION

American higher education has changed dramatically in recent years. A college education is now available to a much broader portion of the socioeconomic spectrum than in years past. The university's role in producing useful knowledge and useful people and in preparing the way for social reform is now universally acknowledged. The fragmentation of scholarly fields into narrower specialties has accelerated, undermining the assumed coherence of broadly conceptual fields like the humanities. The rationale and efficacy of the traditional liberal arts core in undergraduate education have been called increasingly into question. This transformation—now of nearly four decades' duration—continues, and Afro-American studies will necessarily be affected as the American university continues to adapt to changing social, political, economic, and academic conditions and circumstances.

The postwar assumption that the university is an agent of democratic change and an instrument of social reform is now well established and is not likely to be reversed. Demographic changes—specifically those resulting from the ebbing of the tide of applicants produced by the coming-of-age of the postwar "baby boom" generation—are already having effects on college admissions policies, which will in turn have significant consequences on the social mix of future college classes. Many private colleges, competing for their share of shrinking numbers of applicants, are beginning to question (and to modify) the principle of "need-based" financial aid. High tuitions and other college costs have made the greatest impact on middle-class parents and students, and some college administrators have been tempted to shift scholarship funds to merit-based criteria so as to attract the most gifted student applicants. This shift has not been entirely unwelcome to black students and their parents. The great majority of black students now attending private institutions are considered "middle-class," but often only because both parents work full-time to make ends meet. Need-based financial aid formulas place a heavy burden on many parents and force students into considerable debt for their college education. Some among them would benefit from scholarships based on achievement rather than on need.

In any case, rising college costs, reduced federal and state assistance, and smaller numbers of students will make a difference in the number of black students in college, in the socioeconomic background of those who attend, and in the attitude of those students toward their education and the institutions they choose. In the next decade, many black students who might once have attended private colleges will choose state and city institutions instead; many will settle for community or other two-year colleges; many others will be unable to go to college at all. The result is already being felt in all colleges and universities: the return of de facto middle-class higher education. For many scholars and administrators, especially those with unpleasant memories of the tumultuous sixties and seventies, this will be a welcome development.

The earlier crises have passed. Administrators, faculty, and students no longer hear or make demands comparable to those of the 1960s and 1970s. There have been costs, however, particularly to the traditional concept of the liberal arts. The extraordinarily high costs of higher education (especially in the private institutions) have provoked parental and student demands for a clear and immediate payoff. As a result, many colleges have drifted into a preprofessionalism that undermines the traditional concept of general and liberal education. Black parents and students, no less than white, now search for the most direct route to the professional schools. Students may want to study the fine arts, philosophy, music, or literature, but they are quick to give them up in favor of what they think is "good for them" professionally— economics, political science, biology, and so forth. In this sense, Afro-American studies is just one more field perceived by many undergraduates as being of marginal utility. The assumption is, in fact, faulty: most professional schools are indifferent to a student's undergraduate field of concentration; in most instances, a major in Afro-American studies has been considered an asset by admissions officers. But combined parental pressure, personal ambivalence, and overly cautious academic advising tend to push students into the conventional and well-worn paths.

There will, of course, be those students who see their professional careers (in law, government, business, or medicine) as being enriched by a knowledge about blacks in America, and there will be those who follow their tastes and intellectual interests despite the trends. With the political motive no longer compelling, it will be from among this minority of black and white undergraduates that Afro-American studies will draw its students and its future scholars. And programs and departments of Afro-American studies will become more attractive as they bring the most sophisticated methodologies of the social sciences to bear on contemporary black issues and as they enliven discourse in the humanities by the broadening of perspective.

In small Afro-American studies departments and programs, high quality of faculty and teaching will be even more essential to success than it is in larger departments and programs. Great care must be given—more than in conventional and larger departments—to faculty appointments and questions of promotion and tenure.

Needless to say, even one tenured professor who is mediocre or worse can seriously damage or even kill a program. But even poor choices of junior (untenured) faculty may have woeful consequences. Great patience, sustained attention to scholarship and teaching, and a willingness to dismiss marginal faculty even in the face of emotional and political opposition are thus called for. Black and white faculty and administrators must also resist the temptation to make Afro-American studies appointments a substitute for meeting affirmative action goals.

After an increase in the sixties and seventies in the number of blacks entering graduate schools, there has been a sharp drop in the eighties. The increased numbers of blacks pursuing academic careers was an anomaly of the past decade. Earlier, the chances of a black scholar being appointed to the faculty of a northern university were extremely slight—so much so that very few blacks chose to pursue scholarly careers. Projections of the academic job market for the next fifteen or twenty years are not promising for most fields in the humanities and social sciences. High costs and relatively lengthy periods of training for the Ph.D. (seven years on average as opposed to three years for law and two years for business) will push many of the best and brightest black undergraduates into nonacademic fields. The number of blacks enrolled in doctoral programs has been declining and very few blacks are coming forth to fill faculty vacancies. If this trend continues, affirmative action in faculty hiring will be moot as far as blacks are concerned.

Of course, the field of Afro-American studies need not depend on black scholars alone, nor should it. It is desirable, furthermore, that blacks, like other academics, should choose their fields of study on the basis of personal interest and intellectual commitment, not of race. It is nevertheless natural to assume that consequential gains in our knowledge of Afro-American life, history, and culture depend in large part on the presence of significant numbers of black scholars in the humanities and social sciences. The prospect of declining numbers of black scholars

69

thus portends more serious problems for the field than small class enrollments do.

Given the still uncertain status of Afro-American studies departments and programs throughout the country, probably the best institutional support for the development and extension of the field of study will come from one or two centers or institutes of advanced study devoted to the subject. It seems to me that the movement to make academically legitimate the study of a wide range of issues and questions having to do with the black experience in America has been the most valuable outcome of the struggles during the last decade. Afro-American studies will achieve greater impact and influence the more it is permitted to resonate in the conventional disciplines. Standard offerings in history, American literature, economics, political science, and so on should be informed and enriched by scholarship in Afro-American studies.

1. Archibald MacLeish, *The Next Harvard*, Cambridge, Massachusetts: Harvard University Press, 1941.
2. Clark Kerr, *The Uses of the University*, Cambridge, Massachusetts: Harvard University Press, 1963.
3. C. H. Arce, "Historical, Institutional, and Contextual Determinants of Black Enrollment," unpublished doctoral dissertation, University of Michigan, 1976. Cited in Gail E. Thomas, ed., *Black Students in Higher Education: Conditions and Experiences in the 1970s.* Westport, Connecticut: Greenwood Press, 1981, pages 21–23 and passim.
4. Ibid., page 21; cites 1978 Census Bureau data.
5. James A. Perkins, *The University in Transition*, Princeton, New Jersey: Princeton University Press, 1966. The book is composed of lectures delivered at Princeton in 1965.
6. A provocative recent discussion of the plight of the humanities is Walter Jackson Bate's "Crisis of English Studies," *Harvard Magazine* LXXXV (September–October 1982), pages 46–53.
7. Perkins, op. cit., page 22.
8. The assumption was (and is) by no means restricted to predominantly white institutions. If anything, southern black schools have been more insistent on the centrality of the classical and Renaissance tradition of humane letters than northern white schools.
9. Daniel P. Moynihan, *The Negro Family: The Case for National Action*, Washington, D.C.: United States Department of Labor, Government Printing Office, 1965.
10. The significance to blacks of these killings cannot be overstated. In subsequent years, black students bitterly compared the great public outcry at the killing of white students at Kent State to the apparent white indifference to the killing of blacks at Orangeburg.
11. Kenneth B. Clark and Lawrence Plotkin, *The Negro Student at Integrated Colleges*, New York: National

Scholarship Service and Fund for Negro Students, 1963.
12. In terms of adaptability to the institutions and expectations concerning higher education, these class differences are important to note. The sense of class alienation may have been as important in many instances as the sense of racial alienation.
13. See Cleveland Donald, Jr., "Cornell: Confrontation in Black and White," in Cushing Strout and David Grossvogel, eds., *Divided We Stand: Reflections on the Crisis at Cornell,* Garden City, New York: Doubleday, 1970, pages 151–204. This essay provides a rare insight into the workings of black student politics at a time of university conflict.
14. It is probable that four-year liberal arts colleges avoided disruptions over black studies for several reasons. Even with active recruitment, the number of black students remained small. Much student protest, white and black, was against the gigantic, seemingly insensitive and unresponsive university bureaucracy. The smaller four-year college provided an experience on a human scale and encouraged the impression that grievances were listened to and taken into account.
15. *New York Times,* various articles from roughly September 29, 1968, to March 3, 1970. Nathan Hare left San Francisco State in 1970.
16. "Report of the Committee Appointed to Review the Department of Ethnic Studies," 1973. Unpublished. University of California, Berkeley. The history department was quite strong, consisting of Leon Litwack, Lawrence Levine, Winthrop Jordan and others.
17. Armstead L. Robinson et al., *Black Studies in the University,* New Haven: Yale University Press, 1969, page *viii.* Robinson was at the time a senior at Yale College. After earning his Ph.D. in history, he went on to become one of the most respected young black scholars. He currently heads the Afro-American Studies Program and the Carter G. Woodson Institute at the University of Virginia.

18. In addition to Friedel, Social Sciences 5 was taught by Peter Wood, Martin Kilson, and Daniel Fox, with guest lecturers.
19. Henry Rosovsky subsequently served as Dean of the Faculty of Arts and Sciences, from 1974 to 1984.
20. Henry Rosovsky, "What Happened at Harvard," *The American Scholar* XXXVIII (Autumn 1969), pages 562–572.
21. Reported in *Trans-Action* VII (May 1970), page 14.
22. Vincent Harding, "Achieving Educational Equality— Stemming the Black Brain Drain," *Current* CV (March 1969), pages 37–40.
23. Clarke and Plotkin, op. cit., pages 28–39. This study does reveal, however, that the small number of drop-outs in this survey voiced complaints anticipating (mildly and without political intent) black student complaints of the sixties. This may suggest that ob-jective conditions were the same but expectations differed.
24. M. L. Dillon, "White Faces in Black Studies," *Common-weal* XCI (January 30, 1970), pages 476–479.
25. John Blassingame, ed., *New Perspectives on Black Stu-dies,* Champaign, Illinois: University of Illinois Press, 1971.
26. This crisis of identity is by no means unique to black people; witness the upsurge of "ethnicity" in the sixties and seventies.
27. This became a general criticism raised by black and white scholars; for instance, by John Blassingame, op. cit., pages 75–168; by C. Vann Woodward, in "Flight from History," *Nation* CCI (September 20, 1969), pages 142–146 and by Benjamin Quarles.
28. Consider, for instance, the general treatment of W.E.B. DuBois's *Black Reconstruction,* a work that eventually brought about a general revision of the history of that period.
29. Carter G. Woodson, *The Mis-Education of the Negro,* Washington, D.C.: AMS Press, 1933; W.E.B. DuBois, "The Field and Function of the Negro College," in Her-

bert Aptheker, ed., *The Education of Black People: Ten Critiques 1906–1960*, Amherst, Massachusetts: University of Massachusetts Press, 1973, pages 83–92.

30. Wilson Record, "Can Black Studies and Sociology Find Common Ground?" *Journal of Negro Education* CLIV (Winter 1975), pages 63–81; Morris Janowitz and James Blackwell, eds., *The Black Sociologists*, Chicago, Illinois: Chicago Center for Afro-American Studies and Research, 1973; Joyce A. Ladner, ed., *The Death of White Sociology*, New York: Random House, 1973; other divisions are in psychology, political science, and African studies.

31. Harry Edwards, *Black Students*, New York: Free Press, 1970. The quotes are from the dust jacket, which contains proposed curricula for black studies. See also Nathan Hare, "The Sociological Study of Racial Conflict," *Phylon* XXXIII (Spring 1972), pages 27–31.

32. The strengths in history had to do with the fact that Afro-American history was a lively and developing area in American history. Black scholars, of course, and many whites—Leon Litwack, Winthrop Jordan, Eugene Genovese, Herbert Gutman, August Meier, Lawrence Levine, etc.—were building reputations in the field.

33. Maulana Ron Karenga, "The Black Community and the University: A Community Organizer's Perspective," in Robinson, op. cit., pages 37–54.

34. Wesleyan appointed a new chairman/director in 1981: Robert O'Meally, a fine scholar with strong academic interests. He plans to establish a strong program with interdepartmental cooperation. The center remains quasi-independent, however, and it has withstood, because of student loyalty, past attempts at reform.

35. The Afro-American Studies program at UCLA, for instance, is a quasi-institute. It offers no instructional courses but provides means for research for graduate students and postdoctoral scholars.

36. My information about IBW comes from the pamphlet "About the Institute of the Black World" and from

manuscript reports, copies of which are in my possession.

37. National Council for Black Studies, *Black Studies Core Curriculum,* Bloomington, Indiana: National Council for Black Studies, 1982, pages 4–7.

38. Undergraduates also report considerable parental pressure to follow courses of study with a "payoff." Black students, often able to attend college only as a result of great sacrifice by their parents, are especially susceptible to parental pressure to make their education "practical."

39. Blassingame, op. cit., "Black Studies, an Intellectual Crisis," pages 149–168. See also his "Model of an Afro-American Studies Program," ibid., pages 229–239.

40. In the winter of 1984, the dean of the faculty at the University of California at Riverside recommended the disestablishment of the black studies department, Chicano studies, as well as some other small departments. The justification was both economic and academic. UC Riverside has been an economically marginal unit of the UC system. It is as yet unclear whether the recommendation to disestablish will be approved.

41. Cleveland State University requires, for the A.B., four semester courses in Afro-American studies. The courses are well attended and the students (white and black) seem to accept the requirement without undue complaint.

42. By this I mean enrollment for academic rather than political reasons. In the mid-seventies, many black students took courses to "support the program," voting with their feet, as it were. That phase is past.

43. The claim is made by white conservatives at Harvard despite the fact that all black students fall well within the range of all those admitted to the college.

44. Community action programs and all such practical work are not much valued by traditional academics, who tend to regard them as activities of questionable merit for undergraduate training. On this question of community work and black studies, see Kenneth B.

Clark, "A Charade of Power," *Antioch Review* XXIX (Summer 1969), pages 145–148, and Stephen Lythcott's rejoinder, ibid., pages 149–154.

APPENDIX

The following is a selected list of course offerings from the catalogs of several colleges and universities, indicating the variety, and range of courses offered under the rubrics of Afro-American studies, black studies, and African-American studies. When possible and relevant, course descriptions as well as course titles have been provided. The listings are based on catalogs for 1984–85.

Readers are reminded that course titles and even course descriptions may tell little about actual course content and character. This list, therefore, should not be regarded as definitive. One can observe several things, nonetheless: (1) Some departments and programs offer their own courses, while others make up their course offerings through other departments; (2) Some departments and programs give greater weight to the social sciences, others to the humanities; some to practical, per-formance-, or community-oriented courses, others to more purely academic topics; (3) Some departments and programs depend on the institution's broader course offerings to provide their students with a general education, while a few expect their students to be educated entirely within the black studies curriculum; (4) Some departments and programs provide the college or university with service courses such as African language courses, while others do not.

ATLANTA UNIVERSITY

AFRO-AMERICAN STUDIES:

501 Introduction to Afro-American Culture
Introduction to fundamental problems in Afro-American culture.

502 Approaches to the Black Experience
Black experiences are examined and subjected to pragmatic and idealistic criticism.

510 Blacks in the Caribbean
An ethnohistorical approach to the study of Caribbean blacks.

530 Comparative Black Literature
A study of Afro-Romance and Afro-American literature.

535 Afro-American Folklore
A survey of Afro-American folklore in a social and historical context.

540 Introduction to Sea Island Studies
An overview of the history and customs of the Sea Island areas of South Carolina and Georgia and the adjacent mainland areas.

545 The African Continuum
An examination of the persistence of African culture among black populations outside Africa.

550 Afro-American Music
The principal forms and characteristics of Afro-American music.

560 African Art
A survey of the basic forms and styles of black African art.

620 W.E.B. DuBois
A study of several aspects of his work and thought.

UNIVERSITY OF CALIFORNIA (BERKELEY)

DEPARTMENT OF AFRO-AMERICAN STUDIES:

20 Introduction to Afro-American Social Institutions
The sociology of the Afro-American experience through an analysis of the educational, political, religious, economic, and familial dimensions of Afro-American life.

101 Research Methods for Afro-American Studies
Introduction to quantitative methods with special emphasis on survey research techniques and procedure.

109 The Sociology of Communal Politics
An examination of the conditions under which communal groups become politically mobilized.

110a Afro-American Economic History
Emphasis on issues influencing the development of a black economic base in America from 1619 to 1918.

110b Afro-American Economic History
From 1918 to the present.

111 Race, Class, and Gender in the United States
Emphasis on social history and comparative analysis of race and gender relations in American society.

112a Politics and Economic Development in the Third World
Examination of Third World underdevelopment and the broad spectrum of theoretical positions put forward to explain it.

112b Politics and Economic Development in the Third World
A critical appraisal of the modernization policies employed by Third World nations.

113 Race, Ideology, and Economics in Africa and Afro-America
Relationship between the rise of racism as a systematic ideology and slave economics; how racism has been perpetuated and sustained through history in response to national and intranational economic needs.

115 Pan-Africanism: Past and Present

Examination of the concept of Pan-Africanism and its historical and intellectual development.

122 *Black Families in American Society*
Examines the historical roles and functions of families and the development of black people in America from slavery to the present.

123 *Afro-American Religion: Historical Perspectives*
A survey of the religious life of Afro-Americans from the transmission of African religious beliefs during slavery to the present-day black church.

125 *Law and the Black Community in the United States*
An examination of the legal decisions and procedures that have affected the status of blacks in America.

126 *Education and Inequality in American Society*
An examination of the evolution and function of public schools as an American institution, focusing on the policies and practices that have affected the education of black Americans and other racial minorities.

127 *Topics in Black Community Development*
Special topics in the black community are examined, including aging, adolescence, intelligence, etc.

131 *Caribbean Societies and Cultures*
A comparative study of Spanish-, Dutch-, English-, and French-speaking Caribbean societies.

132 *Psychology and Black People: Current Issues*
Examines psychological research and theory pertaining to black people.

133 *Black Children and Youth: Psychological Development*
Examination of the growth and development of the black child through adolescence.

134 *Afro-American Language Patterns*
The structure and development of Afro-American linguistic forms with emphasis on their historical, descriptive, and comparative dimensions.

135 *Caribbean Ethnohistory*
Ecological study of Caribbean slave quarters and maroon communities.

136 *Health, Medicine, and Culture*
Examination of the theoretical issues in medical anthropology. Comparative analysis of the evolution of Afro-American and Caribbean medical traditions.

144 *Religion and Culture in Black America*
Investigation of the varied social and cultural forms of black religious life in America.

150a*Black American Literature, 1746 to 1920*
Introduces the early literary creations and thought of black America.

150b*Black American Literature, 1920 to Present*
Survey of black American literature from the Harlem Renaissance to the present.

CORNELL UNIVERSITY

AFRICANA STUDIES AND RESEARCH CENTER:

131 *Swahili*
Beginning Swahili; grammar, part 1.

132 *Swahili*
Elementary reading and continuation of grammar.

133 *Swahili*
Advanced study in reading and composition.

134 *Swahili*
Advanced study in reading and composition.

137 *Afro-American Writing and Expression*
Designed to promote clear and effective communication skills, using black-oriented materials as models for writing assignments and oral discussions.

138 *Applied Writing Methods on Afro-American Topics*
A writing skills course that explores traditional and nontraditional research sources, using Afro-American experiences as the primary subject matter.

171 *Infancy, Family, and the Community*
Survey of key psychological dimensions of the black experience, covering such issues as race and intelligence, black identity, black family structure, black English, black middle class, and the nature of black psychology.

172 *Teaching and Learning in Black Schools*
Devoted to the history and contemporary issues of black education, such as the struggle for black studies, development of black grammar, and problems of public schools in black communities.

190 Introduction to Modern African Political Systems
This course directs attention to the salient characteristics of Africa's political systems and assesses the way they impinge on development efforts.

202 Swahili Literature
Students gain mastery over spoken Swahili and are introduced to the major Swahili literary forms.

203 History and Politics of Racism and Segregation
The patterns of racism and segregation are dealt with in a historical context, using Southern Africa and North America as case histories.

219 Issues in Black Literature
An examination of literature written for black children. Students write a pamphlet containing their essays, fiction, and poetry and compile a bibliography of literature for black children.

231 Black Political Thought in the United States
An introductory course that will review and analyze the major political formulations developed and espoused by black people in the struggle for liberation.

283 Black Resistance: South Africa and North America
A study of black political movements in South Africa and North America.

285 Black Drama
An introduction to the history of black drama, dramaturgical criticism, and production techniques.

290 The Sociology of the Black Experience
An introductory course on the sociology of the black experience and the field of Afro-American studies.

301 Seminar: Psychological Aspects of the Black Experience
Existing research is used to raise specific questions about new cultural political awareness in the black community. The focus is on individual conversion experiences within the context of social movements.

303 Blacks in Communication Media and Film
The focus is on the general theory of communications, the function of media in an industrialized society, and the social, racial, and class values implied in the communication process.

344 Neocolonialism and Government in Africa
The course is designed to explain why Africa's public administrations in the postcolonial era have generally failed to move from the colonialist ethos to becoming primary instruments for initiating and guiding the process of development.

346 *African Socialism and Nation Building*
An exploration and critical analysis of the various theories of African socialism as propounded by theorists and practitioners.

350 *The Black Woman: Social and Political History*
This course addresses the social organizations, political protests, and political ideologies of black women in the United States, from slavery to the 1980s.

351 *Politics in the Afro-Caribbean World: An Introduction*
A study of the social, political, economic, and psychological forces that have shaped Caribbean societies.

352 *Pan-Africanism and Contemporary Black Ideologies*
A historical study of Pan-Africanism that reviews and analyzes the literature and activities of early black Pan-African theorists and movements.

360 *Ancient African Nations and Civilizations*
An introduction to African history beginning with early civilizations in pre-European Africa.

361 *Afro-American History (from African Background to the Twentieth Century)*
Designed to explore major themes of the black historical experience in America from African origin to the twentieth century.

370 *Afro-American History: The Twentieth Century*
An exploration of major themes of the black historical experience in America during the twentieth century.

381 *Contemporary African History*
A survey of the present problems on the African continent as they appear from 1500 to the present time.

382 *Comparative Slave Trade of Africans in the Americas*
The focus is on eighteenth- and nineteenth-century slave societies in Virginia and South Carolina and eighteenth-century slave societies in the Caribbean.

400 *Political Economy of Ideology and Development in Africa*
This course explores the processes of the historical underdevelopment of Africa.

405 *Political History of the Age of Booker T. Washington and W.E.B. DuBois*
A review of the intellectual and political history of the black United States experience from 1890 to the eve of World War II.

410 *Black Politics and the American Political System*
The course is designed to engage students in a survey and analysis of the theoretical and empirical basis of black politics in America.

420 *Social Policy and the Black Community in the Urban Economy*
Examination of the social, political, and economic factors contributing to the development and perpetuation of the so-called ghetto.

422 *African Literature*
A detailed study of twentieth-century fiction from English-speaking and French-speaking sub-Saharan Africa.

431 *History of Afro-American Literature*
An extensive examination of the impact that Afro-American literature has had on describing, explaining, and projecting the Afro-American experience.

432 *Modern Afro-American Literature*
A study of fiction by modern black writers, focusing on the political and sociological factors that influenced the development and growth of black writing.

460 *History of African Origins of Major Western Religions*
The course is designed to develop an understanding of the basic origins of the teachings responsible for Judaism, Christianity, and Islam.

475 *Black Leaders and Movements in Afro-American History*
A comprehensive analysis of the personalities, ideas, and activities central to the struggle for Afro-American liberation, ranging from the eighteenth century to the present time.

484 *Politics, Conflict, and Social Change in South Africa*
The course examines the history of the African liberation movement from the post–World War II era to the present.

485 *Racism, Social Structure, and Social Analysis Seminar*
An examination of the social structure of American society and the relationship of racial and class categories to social stratification.

490 *Advanced Reading and Research Seminar in Black History*
Designed to help acquaint students with the available sources of information and materials in black history.

495 *Political Economy of Black America*
An examination of the role that black labor has played in the historical development of monopoly, capitalism, and imperialism.

500 *Political Theory, Planning, and Development in Africa*
The course explores the processes of underdevelopment of Africa from the epoch of slavery through colonial and neocolonial phases of domination.

510 *Historiography and Sources: The Development of Afro-American History*
Through a critical examination of the approach, methodology, and

philosophy of major writers in this field, the evolution of Afro-American history is traced from its origin to the present.

550 *Transnational Corporations in Africa and Other Developing Countries*
Examines the role of transnational enterprises as an economic and political factor in the Third World, their relations with the host government, and their interaction with both the private and public sectors of the economy of the host country.

571 *Seminar: Psychological Issues in the Black Community*
A critical examination of existing theory and research on identity development and identity transformation in Afro-American life.

HARVARD UNIVERSITY

AFRO-AMERICAN STUDIES:

103 *Social Analysis of Racial Inequality in the United States*
Surveys the historical origin and subsequent development of racial income inequality in the United States.

105 *Public Policy in Divided Societies*
Examines policy issues having to do with the management of conflict between sub-national population groups divided along racial, ethnic, religious, and/or linguistic lines.

118d *Afro-American History*
The history of the Afro-American people from their African origins to the present. This course examines that story within the context of the developing American nation, its institutions, and its culture.

120 *Conference Course: Race and Race Relations in American History*
This seminar examines the intellectual origins and development of race theory as it pertains to the Afro-American experience.

121 *Black Urban Communities*
Examination of the impact of policies adopted and implemented by local, state, and national public-sector institutions on the political development of black urban communities.

126 *The Black Church and its Music*
Study of the music of the black church through an examination of its congregational songs and formal music.

131a *Afro-American Literature to the 1920s*
A study of major Afro-American writers in the context of American cultural history. I. Black literature and folk culture under slavery. II. "Post-bellum pre-Harlem."

131b Afro-American Literature From the 1930s to the Present
A study of major Afro-American writers in the context of American cultural history. III. From Harlem Renaissance to Federal Writer's Project. IV. Contemporary literature.

133 The Afro-American Folk Arts
Analysis of representative examples of Afro-American folk music, dance, art, tales, poetry, sermons, speech, and theater.

135 History of Afro-American Music
Historical survey of Afro-American music from colonial times to the present; emphasis upon its distinctive features and influence upon Western music.

137 Black Women Writers
The course focuses on the work of Zora Neale Hurston, Toni Morrison, Alice Walker, and others.

138 Conference Course: The Jazz Tradition
Analysis and discussion of the history of classic jazz performance, styles, and artists. Guest lectures and presentations by major jazz artists of representative styles.

146 Black and Puerto Rican Politics: A Comparative Approach
This course focuses on the political experiences of Puerto Ricans in the continental United States. It compares the electoral behavior of blacks and Puerto Ricans in New York City, Chicago, and Boston.

148 Images in the Afro-American Cinematic Experience
Traces the changing nature of the black cinematic experience, analyzing the way in which stereotypical images of the past have been replaced by more complex contemporary characterizations.

150 Conference Course: Martin Luther King
This seminar focuses on the life and ideology of the most well-known leader of the active phase of the civil rights movement.

195 The Politics of Urban Education
Political issues in education that are relevant to Afro-Americans and discussion of how these issues develop and are resolved.

UNIVERSITY OF ILLINOIS (CHICAGO)

BLACK STUDIES:

101 Introduction to Black Studies
Historical and contemporary experiences of Afro-American people. Topics include historiography, economics, racism, and liberation struggles.

103 *Visual Studies in Black Culture*
Introduction to the aesthetic, artistic, and visual imagery produced by Afro-American culture.

105 *Introduction to Black Culture*
The lifestyles and values of ancient and modern black people; adaptation of African culture to the New World.

120 *Introduction to Black Religion*
The literature of the black church and exposure to its living symbols, African influence, music, and preaching.

121 *The Preaching of the Black Church*
The central role of the preacher in the life of the black church; emphasis on the importance of mythology and symbol.

122 *The Music of the Black Church*
Emphasis on spirituals and urban gospel music.

130 *Black Identity: Introduction to Black Psychology*
Historical analysis of the social and psychological dimensions of black identity.

132 *The Black Family in the United States*
Analysis and interpretation of the relationship between racial oppression and family structure and functions.

140 *Techniques of Black Creative Writing*
The relationship between Afro-American culture and literary styles.

141 *Introduction to African History*
Introduction to history and historical methods through the study of African history.

150 *The Black Novel: African, Caribbean, North American*
The study and analysis of selected Afro-American, African-Caribbean, and continental African novels.

151 *Introduction to African Literature*
Introduction to African narratives, poetry, and drama; the social context and performance function of folk tales, myths, and poetry.

154 *The Black Woman as a Writer*
Thematic concerns expressed by the black female in literature; emphasis on conceptual and stylistic patterns of development.

159 *Jazz Laboratory Ensemble*
Practical experience in the preparation and performance of jazz compositions and arrangements.

160 *Black Liberation Movement in America: 1954 to 1974*
Topics include desegregation, civil rights, black power, and political and economic reform movements.

161 *Race to Power: Apartheid in Southern Africa*
The impact of apartheid on the cultural, political, social, and economic development of black South Africans.

205 *Introduction to Black Folklore*
The concepts, theories, and comparative methods of folklore-studies.

216 *Political and Social Philosophy*
Theories on how to evaluate laws and explain the obligation to obey the law.

221 *Black Religious Experiences in Chicago*
Comparative study of history, aesthetics, theology, social consciousness, and cultural values of black religious groups in Chicago.

241 *African History to 1690*

243 *African History: 1640 to 1881*

245 *African History: 1881 to the Present*

247 *Afro-American History to 1850*

248 *Afro-American History from 1850 to 1900*

249 *Afro-American History Since 1900*

250 *Slave Literature*
Afro-American literature during the eighteenth and nineteenth centuries, emphasizing the specific aspects of traditional culture.

251 *Cultural Values in African Literature*
Selected writings by African people in Africa and the Americas.

260 *Black Nationalism in the United States.*
Analysis and interpretation of the nature, cause, and consequences of black nationalist movements.

269 *Africans in Latin America and the Carribbean*
A country-by-country historical study of the peoples of African origin in Latin America and the Caribbean.

271 *Black Women Freedom Fighters in America*
A study of the critical role of black women in the struggle for Afro-American liberation.

280 *Introduction to Research in Black Studies*
Introduction to philosophy, logic, and methods of social science research in black studies.

297 *History of Minorities in the United States: Reconstruction to the Present*
Racial, ethnic, religious, and political minorities in the United States.

350 The Harlem Renaissance
Intellectual thought, poetry, fiction, music, and art of the black cultural resurgence of the 1920s.

OBERLIN COLLEGE

BLACK STUDIES DEPARTMENT:

101 Introduction to the Black Experience
Interdisciplinary exploration of key aspects of black history, culture, and life in Africa and the Americas.

103 Traditional African Cosmology
An introductory survey of African philosophical and metaphysical traditions, including an examination of traditional African religions, spirituality, applied metaphysics, and cultural patterns.

141 The Heritage of Black American Literature
A survey of black American literature from its inception in the eighteenth century to the Harlem Renaissance in the 1920s.

182 Education and the Black Community
To acquaint students with a ghetto scholar's philosophy and methodology for eliminating white and black racism and reducing discrimination and oppression.

201 Afro-American History to 1865
A survey of the cultural, social, and political development of African people in the United States from their pre-seventeenth-century origins to the end of the Civil War.

202 Afro-American History Since 1865
Analysis of Afro-American history from the Reconstruction Era to the rise of Black Power.

203 African History
Survey of the development of African civilization from the earliest beginnings of humanity to the dawn of colonialism.

204 African History
African history from colonialism to the era of independence and neocolonialism.

205 Ethiopianism
In-depth analysis of Ethiopianist beliefs and black American thought from the era of the American Revolution to World War II.

230 American Interaction with Black Africa in the 19th and 20th Centuries
Course investigates the nature and scope of relations between Africans and Americans of African descent. It is a survey of Afro-

American interests and interactions with the African continent over the last two centuries.

232 *The Colonized Mind*
Designed to identify and discuss the processes by which the black mind has become enslaved within the American social and political system.

234 *African Liberation Movements*
Contemporary struggles against white minority rule in Southern Africa. An in-depth analysis of the dynamics and personalities of nationalist movements in Southern Africa.

237 *Black Performances*
Black performance workshop. Course seeks to develop myth-makers of the black experience who can apply sound, form, or movement in an effective narration in either written or perform-ance modes.

238 *Black Arts Workshop*
The workshop combines theory and performance in the areas of radio drama, news and sports reporting, creative writing, dance, and particularly drama.

239 *Black Performance in the Americas*
A quasi-historical, quasi-anthropological look at the performance roles of the New World African from 1619 to the 1980s.

241 *Afro-American Politics*
An analysis of black political theory in the United States.

242 *Modern Black American Literature*
A survey of black American writers beginning with the Harlem Renaissance in the 1920s to the present.

271 *Practicum in Public Schooling*
Students serve as tutors and/or aides in a public school system.

311 *History of Black Nationalism in America*
An examination of the various forms of black nationalism as espoused by Afro-Americans from approximately 1800 to 1900.

312 *History of Black Nationalism*
Analysis of black nationalist sentiments and movements from 1900 to the present.

314 *Garvey and Garveyism*
An examination of the life and times of Marcus Garvey.

317 *Black Pedagogy*
The principal aim of this course is to maximize students' chances of becoming a teacher who is able to help ghetto children obtain high scores on the SATs and read critically *The New York Times*.

343 *Langston Hughes and the Black Aesthetic*
Selected poetry and prose by Hughes, including his autobiography, *The Big Sea*, and his last book of poems, *The Panther and the Lash*.

351 *Pro-Seminar on the Black Novel*
An intensive critique of fiction by black writers, identifying unique and recurring themes, social and psychological content, and variations and similarities in craftsmanship, style, and character.

SAN FRANCISCO STATE UNIVERSITY

BLACK STUDIES:

111 *Black Cultures and Personalities*
An examination of cultural influence on the development of black personality configurations.

200 *Introduction to Black Psychology*
An introductory survey of the theories, characteristic methodologies, and applicability of these methodologies to African-American behavioral experiences.

206 *Black Child Development*
Analysis of traditional theoretical approaches to the study of black children and innovative approaches currently being developed.

210 *Introduction to Black Literature*
A critical analysis of the role of literature in formulating, maintaining, and articulating cultural ethos.

214 *Written Composition in Black Studies*
Development of expository and analytical writing skills within the context of black literature.

215 *Introduction to Black Families*
Introduction to theories and research on American black families. Special attention given to emerging trends in social science literature on black families.

217 *African Rhythm and Drum Expression*
Basic forms and functions of Congolese and other African music.

221 *Afro-American Music: A Twentieth-Century Survey*

225 *Images and Issues in Black Visual Media*
A historical and developmental survey of black film.

230 *Introduction to Afro-American Theater*

300 *From Africa to America*
Early African civilization and the precolonial era.

301 *Africa in Global Perspective*
Exploration of physical, social, cultural, political, economic, and

business environments of Africa.

302 *Black Diaspora*
Dynamics of black dispersal, fifteenth to twentieth centuries.

303 *Afro-American History*
Emphasis on recurrent themes and issues in black history since the nineteenth century.

310 *Anthropology of Blackness*
A review and critique of traditional anthropological theories and methodologies as they relate to understanding black peoples.

320 *Black Politics, Mass Movements, and Liberation Themes*
Political constructs and basic premises that draw upon political experiences of black people.

326 *Black Religion*
Examination of the philosophical basis of the contemporary black religious movement.

330 *Sociological Dimensions of the Black Experience*
Sociological dimensions of the black experience are examined to develop an appreciation of the tentative nature of human knowledge.

340 *The Economics of the Black Community*
Economic problems of black people. The role of black labor in the American capitalistic economy.

370 *Health, Medicine, and Nutrition in the Black Community*
A study of the dietary and health practices of black people.

375 *Law in the Black Community*
An investigation of city, state, and federal laws and how they affect the human rights, self-determination, and survival of the black community in America.

376 *Government, the Constitution, and Black Citizens*
The nature and source of the constitutional power of federal and state government, especially in regard to issues involving poor and black citizens.

400 *Black Arts and the Humanities*
Examination of the creative efforts of black writers, artists, etc.

410 *Literature of Blackness*
Black experience as presented by major black writers.

411 *African, African-American Literature*
Examines the literature of blacks of two continents and analyzes the critical impact of American black authors on African writing and perspective.

420 Black Fiction: Major Contributions of Black Fiction
Considered in relation to the development of black political traditions in prose style.

425 Islam in Black Communities
An overview of the growth and development of the religions of Islam in American black communities. Focuses on the personal teachings of such people as Ali, Elijah Muhammed, Malcolm X.

430 Black Poetry
An examination of the structure, style, and technique of representative black poets.

440 Black Oratory
Oratory as part of the black American's political, social, and intellectual history.

450 Black Philosophy
The foundation of black philosophy from ancient Africa to the present.

500 Black Involvement in Scientific Development
Introduction to scientific development, stressing the contributions of black scientists.

515 Black Family Studies
The structure, history, and function of the black family. Particular emphasis is placed on the African cultural tradition as related to black family life.

550 Issues in Black Psychology
Seminar on special psychological issues concerning black people in America.

551 Field Work in Black Studies
Supervised field work in community organizations.

555 Pigmentation and the Experience of Color
Historical and contemporary research focusing on the functional relationship between pigmentation and the African-American experience.

560 Black Counseling
Counseling and problems of the black child are studied.

605 Arts and Politics of the Black Experience
Explores major Afro-American cultural achievements in the performing, literary, and visual arts.

610 Arts, Myth, and Religion
The interrelationship between African art and culture as a reflection of social values and religious processes.

611 Politics of Religion

The interrelationships between religion and culture in Africa; religion as a reflection of social values.

617 *Black Dance Experience*
Traditional and contemporary dance forms of Central African nations.

620 *The Music of Blackness I*
Analysis of styles and techniques of major traditions of black music.

621 *The Music of Blackness II*
For the serious student who wants to perform professionally either in the recording studio or on stage.

622 *Evolution of Afro-American Music*
A philosophical exploration of Afro-American music, from its African roots to its diverse present expressions.

STANFORD UNIVERSITY

PROGRAM OFFERINGS IN AFRICAN AND AFRO-AMERICAN STUDIES:

59a,b,c. Dance Theater Production

82a,b,c. Gospel Choir Workshop

105 *Introduction to African and Afro-American Studies*
An introduction to African and Afro-American studies as an interdisciplinary field.

113 *Western Culture and the Black Diaspora—The Semiotics of Self and Other*
Narrative analysis of selected texts to examine the significations accorded Africa, the "Negro," and the Black Diaspora in the signification system of Western culture.

114 *Africa and the Black Diaspora: An Introduction to its Literature, Thought, and Cultural Worlds*
A general introduction to the parallelisms and differences in the literature, thought, and cultural worlds, both of contemporary Africa and the African-descended communities in the New World.

115 *Ancient African History: The Truth Revealed*
Explores the African origins of humanity, emphasizing ancient African societies and civilizations, specifically those of Ethiopia, Egypt, and West Africa.

126 *Black Perspectives in Medicine*
Through readings, discussions, and contact with black doctors and other health care professionals, this course examines the role of blacks in medicine and issues specific to their health care services.

127 *Black Perspectives in Engineering*
Examines the roles of and opportunities available to blacks in engineering and other technical fields.

130 *Coding Differences: Race/Class/Sex/Culture/I.Q. and the Gender Model as Functions of the Contemporary Human System*
Examines the use made of the analogy of gender—i.e., biological differences—to code socially produced differences as natural differences.

162e *Introduction to Caribbean Poetry: English, French, Spanish*
Focuses on the literature of the former French and British islands.

165 *Afro-Hispanic Culture and Literature*
Concentration on Spanish-speaking countries with a sizable black population, particularly Colombia and Cuba.

248 *The Caribbean-Americas: An Introduction to Their Literature, Thought, and Cultural Worlds*

YALE UNIVERSITY

AFRO-AMERICAN STUDIES PROGRAM:

123a *American Race Relations*
A survey of racial ideologies in America, theories of race and racism, and contemporary patterns of race relations.

130b *Introduction to African Oral Traditions and Written Literatures*

131a *Introduction to Afro-American Literature*
Afro-American literature studies through close readings of selected major works.

160b *Afro-American History*

161a *Afro-Americans, from the Beginnings to Emancipation*

162a *Afro-Americans, from Emancipation to the Present*

165a *Introduction to Afro-American Music*
An explication of the North American musical amalgam of seminal European and African performance practices.

178b *From West Africa to the Black Americas: The Black Atlantic Visual Tradition*
Art, music, and the dance in key classical civilizations south of the Sahara and their impact on the rise of New World art and music.

184b *Politics and the Black American*
An overview of the interaction between black Americans and the American political system.

94

200 *Elementary Swahili*

201 *Second-Year Swahili*

202 *Third-Year Swahili*

205 *Elementary Hausa*

206 *Second-Year Hausa*

207 *Third-Year Hausa*

210 *Elementary Yoruba*

211 *Second-Year Yoruba*

212 *Third-Year Yoruba*

224b *Sectionalism, Civil War, and Reconstruction: The United States, 1840-1877*
Focuses on the role of politics in bringing on the Civil War, the war's role in modernizing American society, and the adjustments of planters and former slaves to freedom.

235b *History of Jazz and Its Roots*
A historical survey of American Jazz, beginning with its origins in African music.

250b *Blacks and the Law*
Explores the ways in which legislative and judicial policy have affected the legal and socioeconomic status of Afro-Americans.

258b *Black Folklore*
Afro-American vernacular culture in the Americas.

266a *Race, Ethnicity, and Urban Politics*
The significance of racial and ethnic factors in urban governments in the United States.

330b *The Idea of Race: Pan-Africanism, 1850-1940*
Examines "Pan-Americanism," from its earliest roots in mid-nineteenth-century Afro-American intellectual history to the more mature thought of DuBois.

338b *American Literature: Public Norms and Private Values*
Based on significant groups of black and white American writers, a study of the unfolding negotiation between social authority and individual experience in the matter of defining the world.

340b *Black Discourse in Latin America*
The struggle of African cultures with the religious, social, and legal codes in Latin America, from the eighteenth century onward.

357b *Independence and Its Aftermath in Francophone Black Africa*
Independence as both fulfillment and disillusionment, recaptured past and uncertain present.

378a Masquerades in West Africa

Examination of West African masks and masquerading as transformations and metamorphoses.

425b Psychosocial Study of Black Autobiography

Autobiographies of black men and women analyzed especially for understanding of their coping mechanisms, with attention to problems, satisfactions, disappointment, grief, and fulfillment.

426a Cultural Psychology

Examination of the psychological implications of the unique and shared experiences of Afro-Americans in the United States and in Caribbean nations.

430b Afro-Americans in the Twentieth Century: A Historical Survey

An examination of the social, political, economic, and educational conditions for Afro-Americans in the twentieth century.

432a Race, Ethnicity, and Social Reform

A comparative examination of the major social problems faced by American racial and ethnic groups, and the development of agencies of self-help and reform to deal with those problems.

467a Culture, Class, and the Afro-American Intellectual

Examination of the potential dilemma of activist intellectuals who claim cultural solidarity with the masses, at the same time that their class and educational background separate them from most of their brethren.